Promoting children's learning from birth to five

Promoting children's learning from birth to five

Developing the new early years professional

Angela Anning and Anne Edwards

Open University Press
Buckingham · Philadelphia

Open University Press
Celtic Court
22 Ballmoor
Buckingham
MK18 1XW

e-mail: enquiries@openup.co.uk
world wide web: http://www.openup.co.uk

and
325 Chestnut Street
Philadelphia, PA 19106, USA

First Published 1999

A catalogue record of this book is available from the British Library

ISBN   0 335 20217 9 (hb)   0 335 20216 0 (pb)

Library of Congress Cataloging-in-Publication Data
Anning, Angela, 1944–
    Promoting children's learning from birth to five : developing the
new early years professional / Angela Anning and Anne Edwards.
        p. cm.
    Includes bibliographical references and index.
    ISBN 0–335–20217–9. – ISBN 0–335–20216–0 (pbk.)
    1. Early childhood education – Great Britain.   2. Early childhood
education – Great Britain – Curricula.   3. Early childhood teachers –
Training of – Great Britain.   I. Edwards, Anne, 1946– .
II. Title.
LB1139.3.G7A55   1999
372.21'0941–dc21   99–14376
                                                                              CIP

Typeset by Graphicraft Limited, Hong Kong
Printed in Great Britain by Biddles Ltd, Guildford and King's Lynn

Contents

Introduction

Early years workers, wherever they are based and however different their roles, have demanding jobs. Current emphases on children's entitlement to educational opportunities have added to these demands and have highlighted the diverse training and experiences of early years professionals. We have always believed that the rich mix of professional expertise found in pre-school provision has been a strength to be tapped. The research project that underpins this book demonstrates the strength of the mix of expertise and shows how professionals from a university, three local authorities and a wide range of backgrounds and settings worked together to develop materials and strategies which aimed at supporting very young children as learners.

This book has three major themes:

- an exploration of the development of a pre-school *community of understanding* through a research partnership between local authorities, practitioners and university-based early years specialists;
- an examination of how enquiring practitioners who work from evidence are able to give strong, interactive and sensitive support to young children as they learn in the areas of early literacy and mathematics;
- a focus on children as learners from birth to 5 as they learn to become people who want to learn.

Our exploration of these themes brings us to consider ways of working with parents; how to support the learning of colleagues; how to manage long-term change; current research on early literacy and mathematical thinking; and how to provide environments in which children are well-supported as learners and adults are able to interact responsively with them.

The title of this book shows that our focus is on young children and their learning. But we are convinced that children will learn most readily in situations where adults are keen to learn and take nothing for granted. Preparing young children to be the learners that their futures will require them to be is a responsible job. We found the blend of expertise available in our research partnership to be an exhilarating mix and are confident that, together, early childhood professionals can meet the challenges facing them. Early childhood provision already has a strong professional base. In this book we explore the strength of that base and the support that it can provide for young learners.

The book draws on a project we ran together and is an enterprise for which we are jointly responsible. We each took the lead on specific chapters and commented on each others' work. Angela Anning led on Chapters 1, 2, 5, 6 and 10 and Anne Edwards on Chapters 3, 4, 7, 8 and 9. Throughout the text we argue for collaboration and knowledge construction through joint activity. The project and the book have been such an experience for us.

We are, however, particularly grateful to the following people for their collaboration and the knowledge they shared: Jean Barker, Jan Bell, Mary Brailsford, Maureen Brett, Vanessa Broadbent, Margaret Buckley, Cilla Carr, Angela Clarke, Margaret Clarke, Margaret Fairclough, Anne-Marie Graham, Jean Hayes, Julie Helm, Ann Langston, Jill Lee, Jackie Lincoln, Judy MacDonald, Maureen McGlynn, Andrea Nicholson, Randolph Prime, Irena Riley, Sonia Roberts, Basil Sage, Peggy Sleight, Fiona Taylor, and Irene Vickers.

We are also grateful to Deborah Brady, Nicky Hutchinson, Pat Russell and Sarah Warm (née Boyes) for the administrative and secretarial support for the project and related publications.

① Setting the national scene

⚪ The research project

The two-year period of the research project on which this book is based (January 1997 to September 1998) was a challenging time for those working in and for services for young children in the United Kingdom (UK). It was the period in which a new curriculum framework, *Desirable Outcomes for Children's Learning on Entering Compulsory Education* (DfEE/ SCAA 1996a) was introduced to all settings with 4-year-olds on roll. There was considerable anxiety among early years practitioners, particularly those in the care sector, about putting the framework into practice and about preparing for the system of national inspections set up to monitor the implementation of the *Desirable Outcomes* model in the wake of a short-lived voucher scheme entitling parents of all 4-year-olds to nursery education. Anxiety was further exacerbated by the introduction of a baseline assessment statutory requirement for all schools from September 1998. Baseline testing of children leaving their pre-school settings was focused on their achievements at the start of formal schooling in English, mathematics and personal and social development. These national policy changes, which will be discussed in more detail below, meant that curriculum development, especially in literacy and mathematics, was high on the agenda of the development plans of the majority of pre-school settings in England and Wales in 1997–8.

The research project was funded by the departments with responsibility for supporting children's services in three local authorities. The aim was to bring together expertise from key practitioner researchers from a range of types of pre-school and day care settings, with university-based researchers, to develop and articulate a curriculum model for effective education in literacy and mathematics for very young children. The objectives were to:

- describe what strategies educarers use to take advantage of what young children bring to pre-school learning contexts;
- identify strategies for the involvement of parents/carers as active partners in young children's care and education;
- identify what organizational features of pre-school learning contexts maximize the quality of curriculum experiences offered to young learners;
- define the features of adult/child and adult/adult interactions which are effective in promoting children's learning in pre-school settings;
- design curriculum literacy and mathematical development models for early childhood settings with exemplary materials for local contexts;
- develop a team of trainers capable of disseminating project findings at local, national and international levels.

Though the political and policy imperatives resulted in a focus on literacy and mathematics, the long-term aim was that the methods of working we were to trial would provide a model for the development of other aspects of the curriculum for each of the three local authorities. Details of the curriculum model that we constructed between us will be given in Chapters 5 to 8. Details of the methodology of the research project will be given in Chapter 3.

First of all it is important to set out the context in which the project took place and to outline its theoretical underpinning. The theoretical basis for this book draws on sociocultural psychology which emphasizes the relationships between individuals, actions, meanings, contexts, communities and cultural histories (see, for example, Lave and Wenger 1991; Chaiklin and Lave 1993; Wertsch *et al.* 1995). These theories will be discussed in Chapters 3 and 4. We also draw on Bronfenbrenner's ecological model of human development (Bronfenbrenner 1979) to argue the significance of the macro-system – the societal and cultural values and attitudes implicit in the way society organizes work, education and childcare systems – on the micro-systems of adult/child/parent/carer interactions operating in settings catering for young children. Bronfenbrenner's model will be discussed at the end of this chapter. Finally, we argue that it is not possible to interpret current exemplifications of policy into practice without an understanding of their historical/sociocultural precedents (Cooter 1992). So it is to the changes in policy and practice in pre-school education and day care during the last 25 years that we turn first.

Changes in services for young children in the UK during the last 25 years

Pre-school education

In 1972, when Margaret Thatcher was secretary of state for education, a government White Paper, *Education: A Framework for Expansion* (DES

1972), recommended that nursery education should be expanded to provide places for 50 per cent of 3-year-olds and 90 per cent of 4-year-olds. The White Paper argued that nursery education was 'valuable as a means of reducing the educational and social disadvantages suffered by children from homes which are culturally and educationally deprived' (p. 3). The notion of nursery/infant education being about 'social rescue' strongly imbued in the philosophies of the great philanthropists such as Robert Owen, religious groups such as the Church of England, the Methodists and Catholics and innovators in the field such as Montessori and the McMillan sisters (see Anning 1997, Chapter 1) was central to the discourse of the Paper. It also argued, largely on the grounds of economy, but also in the interests of continuity for young children's education, that expansion should take place in nursery classes attached to primary schools rather than within designated nursery schools: 'this avoids a change of school and enables educational development to be planned as a whole from three or four to the beginning of the junior or middle-school course' (DES 1972: 3). So a second key notion was that the purpose of nursery education was to prepare children for school. The very word 'pre-school', which has become common parlance in the UK, enshrines this notion; yet early childhood specialists have argued consistently that education for under-5s should be seen as a phase in its own right (see, for example, Blenkin and Kelly 1996; Moss and Penn 1996) rather than a service preparing children for 'proper' schooling.

In 1988 the Education Reform Act instigated a series of radical changes in the English and Welsh education systems. For the first time, schools were bound by statutory requirements for coverage of a centrally defined National Curriculum and related arrangements for testing. Although statutory schooling was still deemed to begin at the age of 5, early years educators were drawn into the reforms both by whole school requirements to plan with colleagues within a subject-based model of learning and by models of assessing, recording and reporting children's progress which were designed to ensure children's entitlement to continuity in education – a central plank of the arguments for curriculum reform.

Early models of assessment of the revised arrangements for teaching 5- to 7-year-olds emphasized the importance of formative teacher assessments (TAs) on a regular basis in classrooms (see DES 1988). These were to operate alongside the formal assessment requirements, the standard assessment tasks (SATs), controlled by the School Examination and Assessment Council (SEAC) and to be administered at the end of each key stage. It was the early years practitioners in schools – who had the expertise in assessments based on observation and interpretation of evidence of children's learning – who were to characterize TAs. Many nursery teachers and nursery nurses were operating their own sophisticated observation and profiling systems for children in their settings (Bartholemew and

Bruce 1993; Whalley 1994). Others were using systems produced by researchers – for example, the *Keele Pre-school Assessment Guide* (Tyler 1985) or Wolfendale's *All About Me* (Wolfendale 1989) which involved parents and nursery staff recording evidence of children's achievements. Early years practitioners found themselves leading school-based or local education authority in-service staff development sessions on formative assessment. Sadly SATs results soon began to dominate the political agenda as they were seized upon by politicians to construct league tables to identify 'good' and 'bad' schools, particularly punishing Labour dominated inner-city constituencies. Inevitably as teachers and governing bodies responded to the external pressures to perform well in SATs tests, the emphasis in schools drifted away from formative to summative assessment models (see Shorrocks *et al*. 1993 for an analysis of the impact of the first rounds of end of Key Stage 1 SATs, and Gipps 1994 for a more general discussion of the impact on children, teachers and parents of different models of assessment). The gains made in teacher expertise in their early attempts to operate diagnostic TA systems which fed back into curriculum planning were dissipated. This loss of expertise in evidence-based assessment, rather than pencil and paper based testing, had consequences for the models of assessment used by practitioners in pre-school settings.

In 1989 a House of Commons select committee on *Achievement in Primary Schools* (HMSO 1989) recommended that nursery education should be available to all 3- and 4-year-olds whose parents wished to access it. The committee debated the issue of changing the statutory school starting age of 5 years, but decided to retain it. They acknowledged that, where no nursery classes were available, many children were entering primary school reception classes at the age of 4. They recommended:

> Where a nursery class or school does not exist the suitable conditions for admission would be where the infant class conforms to levels appropriate to the age and developmental needs of the child in terms of staffing and equipment, and we recommend that such conditions be fixed by the DES and should compare in all respects, with the requirements of nursery classes.
>
> (HMSO 1989: lxxvii, para. 5.45)

These recommendations were ignored, again in the interest of economy, as more and more children entered full-time schooling at age 4. Research evidence accumulated of inappropriate levels of staffing, pedagogic practices, curriculum activities, physical space and equipment for 4-year-olds in schools (Bennett and Kell 1989; Cleave and Brown 1989, 1991a, 1991b; Pascal 1990). Moreover, because government policy on the expansion of services for under-5s was advisory rather than statutory, local authorities were able to respond arbitrarily to recommendations to improve nursery provision. Some local authorities with an historical legacy of promoting nursery education, such as Salford, Bradford and Newcastle in the North of England, and many of the London boroughs subsumed under the Inner London Education Authority, continued to expand their services for young children; but across the country access to services was patchy. For example, DES statistics in 1990 indicated that 66 per cent of under-5s in Hounslow were attending nursery classes or schools, whereas in Wiltshire only 3 per cent were attending, and none at all in Gloucestershire (DES 1993).

Meanwhile, three influential reports were commissioned to investigate aspects of pre-school education. The Rumbold Committee of Inquiry was an all-party committee set up to investigate the quality of education for 3- and 4-year-olds in England across the diversity of voluntary services, maintained and private education and social services provision. Their findings, set out in 'The Rumbold Report', were that 'access to services is still largely determined by where a child lives, when his or her birthday is, whether parents have access to information about services, and whether they can afford fees where there is no public provision' (DES 1990: 27–8). Two further inquiries were funded by independent agencies. In 1993 *Learning to Succeed* (National Commission on Education 1993), sponsored by the Paul Hamlyn Foundation, recommended that high-quality, publicly-funded education provision should be available for all 3- and 4-year-olds. In 1994, *Start Right: The Importance of Early Learning* (Ball 1994), funded by the Royal Society of Arts, argued that investment in good nursery education was the best investment a nation can make. Yet central government was not sufficiently persuaded to fund an expansion of nursery education.

In the absence of coherent central government or local authority policies on pre-school provision, play groups and independent nursery schools and day care facilities opened where there was local demand. The Pre-School Playgroups Association, begun in the 1960s, provided a support system for many parents, almost always women, to establish playgroups offering part-time, low-cost places for pre-school aged children in rented premises. These were usually shared with other voluntary organizations such as youth clubs, cubs or brownies, and took the form of church or village halls and latterly the spare classrooms of primary schools. The Pre-School Playgroups Association, now the Pre-School Learning Alliance, grew into an influential lobbying group in its own right as women became empowered by working together, under severe financial and practical constraints, to fill the gaps left by inept government leadership in pre-school services. The expansion of private, fee-paying nurseries and childminders escalated in the financial boom time of the 1980s. Between 1980 and 1991, places for children expanded by 16 per cent in playgroups, by 259 per cent in private nurseries and by 137 per cent with childminders (Sylva and Moss 1992). Table 1.1 shows the proportions of

Table 1.1   Under 5s in England: use of services 1975, 1985, 1994

	1975	*1985*	*1994*
Places per 100 children 0–4			
Local authority day nurseries	0.8	1.0	0.69
Private nurseries	0.8	0.8	3.83
Childminders	2.6	4.7	11.05
Places per 100 children 3–4			
Playgroups	23.3	33.8	31.33
Pupils as % of 3- and 4-year-olds			
Nursery schools and class	10.0	22.5	26.40
Under 5s in infant class	18.9	20.7	24.98
Independent school	2.1	2.5	3.69

Source: Early Childhood Unit statistics 1996 compiled from government sources in Pugh (1996a: 12).

young children in different forms of provision in England over the last 25 years.

The influx of 4-year-olds into reception classes in primary schools was further exacerbated by the Conservative government's short-lived voucher scheme for so-called 'nursery' education in 1996. It is significant that though the idea of vouchers for education had figured in the discourse and ideology of the Conservative Party for 20 years, it had been rejected by strong lobbying from male-dominated phases, such as secondary or further education, as unworkable. It was imposed on the 'soft', female-dominated target of pre-school education despite protestations from most of its constituents.

In 1994, John Major, Margaret Thatcher's successor as prime minister, pledged at the Conservative Party Conference that his party would ensure that nursery places would be offered to all 4-year-olds whose parents wanted them. An under-5s task group was set up in the Department for Education and Science to put the pledge into practice. In the spirit of free-market enterprise the expansion of nursery education was intended to be via private and voluntary sector initiatives. The voucher scheme was set up to channel the money to new providers. Every parent received a voucher worth £1100 of 'nursery' education in the run up to the general election in February 1996. The administration of the scheme was contracted to a private company at an estimated cost of £730 million. Playgroup leaders were outraged when, the day after the scheme was launched, it was announced that playgroups would receive only half the cost of each voucher on the grounds that their operating costs were lower. At one stroke the Pre-School Learning Alliance, representing

200,000 playgroups across the country, many of whose stalwarts were Conservative voters, was alienated from the voucher scheme.

In fact, most parents of 4-year-olds opted to 'spend' their vouchers on 'proper' school in the reception classes of primary schools. The Conservative government had been quietly deregulating the health and safety requirements for 'nursery' education in the run up to the introduction of vouchers. Parents were therefore 'conned' into exchanging their vouchers for nursery education for places in reception classes where research and evidence based on the findings of the Office for Standards in Education (Ofsted) had already indicated that provision was often inadequate and/or inappropriate for 4-year-olds. A knock-on effect was that playgroups and nursery schools and classes were left with a much younger population of 2- and 3-year-olds. Managers and grassroots practitioners had to adjust rapidly to accommodate the younger 'clientele' with different staffing ratios, resources, curriculum activities, grouping arrangements and styles of adult/children interaction.

Against this background, the School Curriculum and Assessment Authority (SCAA) was asked to draw up a curriculum framework, *Desirable Outcomes For Children's Learning on Entering Compulsory Education* (DfEE/SCAA 1996a), for 3- and 4-year-old children to be implemented in every setting claiming voucher status. A parallel Department for Education and Employment publication, *The Next Steps* (DfEE/SCAA 1996b) set out arrangements for the administration of the voucher scheme and for a national system of inspecting all providers who, if they wished to claim voucher status, were required to demonstrate that they were delivering the *Desirable Outcomes* curriculum.

In May 1997 the Conservatives were convincingly trounced by Labour in a general election. In the run up to polling day, Tony Blair, the Labour leader, had announced that the 1997 election was about 'Education, Education, Education'. He pledged that the voucher scheme would be dismantled by a Labour government and the money diverted to expand nursery provision. Thus, the voucher scheme was abolished three months after its inception. Within weeks of the election, the new government published a significant White Paper, *Excellence in Schools* (DfEE 1997). The paper proposed clear targets within early childhood education for the year 2002:

- high-quality education for all 4-year-olds whose parents want it;
- an early years forum in every area, planning child care and education to meet local needs;
- a network of early excellence centres to spread good practice;
- effective assessment of all children starting school.

Each local authority was required to set up an early years forum (early years partnership) representing the full range of providers and users of early years education in the area. The partnerships were charged with re-viewing the children's services currently available in their Local Authority area and drawing up early years development plans. The plans were to show how, over time, education would be dovetailed with high-quality child care. It is to the field of child care, where practitioners had been experiencing parallel dramatic changes in policy and practice, that we now turn.

Child care

Public commitment to and investment in day care services during the last 25 years has been equally patchy. Day care provision was not high on the Conservative Party agenda during their 18 years in power. Their policy, underpinned by the ideology of the market-place, was to invite employers to provide day care facilities or to encourage private providers to respond to consumer demand. They also took the ideological stance that parents had the prime responsibility for providing for their children and argued against the idea of the 'nanny state' providing services for children. Gillian Pugh, then of the National Children's Bureau, gave this evidence to the House of Commons in 1989: 'The government believes that in the first instance it is the responsibility of parents to make arrangements, including financial arrangements, for the day-care of pre-school children' (Pugh 1996a: 12).

Ironically, in an era dominated by a radical, reforming woman prime minister, Margaret Thatcher, the dominant male attitude of her party towards child care services and working women remained ambivalent. On the one hand, powerful right-wing lobbies, such as the Institute of Economic Affairs, argued against expanding child care and against encouraging women with young children to work. In a polemical book published by the institute (Morgan 1996), Morgan argued vehemently against the campaign for day care, likening it to 'a juggernaught racing downhill' and against transferring responsibility for child-rearing out of the home and onto 'third-party carers' (p. 125). Echoes of 'proper mothers should be at home with their children' were heard in the dis-course of Conservative Party politicians.

On the other hand, during the last two decades patterns of employ-ment favoured women rather than men. As manufacturing industries declined, service industries expanded. Employers, seeking a more flexible, part-time, cheaper, non-unionized workforce found that women fitted more passively into such patterns of employment than men. Women also traditionally have better 'people skills' and that quality was both useful and profitable for industries serving the public at a face-to-face level. The shifts in employment trends have been gradual, but relentless. In 1951 only 12 per cent of the workforce in England was female. By

1998, the percentage had risen to 30 per cent. In communities where manufacturing industries had employed predominantly men, the loss of jobs, and subsequent upheavals in their family and social lives caused massive levels of stress, disorientation and anger for men.

Today, over half of women with children under 5 work. These trends have resulted in increased demands for day care for young children and account for the rapid expansion of childminding provision indicated in Table 1.1. There has also been a steady rise in the number of single parents (re-labelled in New Labour speak as lone parents) to a level of 1.7 million in 1998, mostly women. In 1998 1 million of these were unemployed or inactive in work. In the early 1990s the Child Support Agency had been set up by the Conservative government. It was designed to provide a structure by which the fathers of the children of lone parents would be assessed financially and required to support their families. Again it was underpinned by the belief that individuals, not the state, should take responsibility for the welfare of children. The agency failed hopelessly to make any significant impact on gaining access to fathers' incomes to support their children and in 1998 it was radically restructured to launch a new initiative to force men to share the responsibility and costs of raising children they had fathered. The New Labour policy was to wean lone parents off state benefits by getting them into work or training under the Welfare to Work initiative. Particularly in urban areas this resulted in a further expansion of both day care and before- and after-school care provision (HMSO 1998). The latter became known as 'wrap-around care'.

Day care has traditionally been the responsibility of social services in the UK. In 1991 the Children Act set out new requirements for local authorities to provide services for 'children in need' and to register, inspect and review child care services. The Act requires local authorities to review services every three years jointly with education authorities and in association with health authorities, voluntary organizations and independent providers. The emphasis is on quality control and accountability both to funding agencies and to 'consumers' of services. Guidance is given on ratios of staff to children, room sizes and space, health and safety, record keeping, disciplining of children and equal opportunities issues (DoH 1991).

In the guidance there is a strong emphasis on partnership with parents/carers and on the importance of offering parents choices in child care. However, parental choice is limited by what services are available. Again the lack of a coherent policy for child care for working parents from central government has resulted in patchy provision. For many parents this means moving their children from one service to another in frantic attempts to cope with the financial and practical demands of working and parenting. This results in an inherent instability in very young children's lives. In a longitudinal study based at the Thomas Coram

Institute, 255 London-based families with their first child were tracked from 1982 to 1988 (Melhuish 1991). Three quarters of the mothers returned to work before their child was 9 months old. Nearly half of the children who were cared for in day care settings experienced at least one change of setting before they reached the age of 3, and a quarter experienced two or more changes (Brannen and Moss 1990).

Even when children stay in the same setting, there is another feature of instability in their lives. Because of poor working conditions and low pay there is often a high turnover of staff in day care settings so that children experience frequent changes of carers. Research into the care and learning needs of children under 3 in day care nurseries based on 150 hours of observation of babies in 15 nurseries in England by Elfer and Selleck (1999), Elfer, Goldschmied and Selleck (1999) of the National Children's Bureau is likely to confirm the frequency of changes in those caring for babies in shift systems and where the turnover of staff is high. It is almost impossible under these conditions for babies and staff to develop authentic emotional relationships. This is deeply worrying when, as we will argue in Chapter 4, children need close and consistent relationships with key adults in their lives in order to thrive both emotionally and cognitively.

In addition to servicing the needs of working parents, there is a second feature of day care which parallels the concept of 'social rescue' embedded in many inner-city nursery education initiatives. Publicly-funded day care, run by local authority social services departments, has a strong emphasis on providing support for children and their families defined as 'in need' or 'at risk'. This has resulted in a concentration of children with emotional and/or learning difficulties in publicly-funded day care settings. In the report of a national, longitudinal survey of all the children born in one week in 1970 in England, Scotland and Wales (Osborn and Milbank 1987) data on the composition of the population attending day nurseries indicated that more than 30 per cent of them were referred by social workers and 80 per cent of the families were experiencing social or family problems. The function of day care provision has thus largely been seen as 'social rescue' and fees for the children's attendance in the day nurseries have often been paid by local authorities. The nurseries have traditionally been staffed by personnel with social work or nursery nurse training backgrounds. Given their population and purposes, their concerns have mainly been for the health, safety and emotional well-being of the children. Until the onset of the voucher scheme, day care staff were not expected to offer an explicitly educational component to the care of the children, though they have traditionally focused on the development of children's competencies in spoken language. Day care settings also have a strong tradition of supporting the needs of the families of the children in their care.

European and Scandinavian services for young children

Bronfenbrenner (1979) argues in his ecological model of child development that societies should place a high value on responding to the needs of young children. But he also argues that this can only be achieved when members of that society acknowledge the complex interrelationship between children, parents, educators, carers, community groups, those with responsibility for employment and housing, etc. In turn, priorities for allocating money to particular aspects of family needs – including the provision of children's services – depend crucially on the value systems of the dominant groups who determine social policy and allocate funding to community or welfare services.

It is useful to remind ourselves that there are different models of provision for young children in other cultural contexts and to point out the features of just one or two examples from other countries. In Denmark, for example, there is a long-standing tradition of prioritizing funding to maintain high-quality services for young children and almost all children in the 0–7 age group attend some form of day care. In 1981 the Danish Child Welfare Commission set out long-term aims for children's services. These were:

- to respect the child as an individual in the family and in society;
- to give the child a central position in the life of grown-ups;
- to promote – in a wider sense – the physical conditions in which young children grow up;
- to promote equal opportunities in the conditions of life of children in both a material and in a cultural sense (quoted in David 1993: 20).

The concepts of social responsibility and democratic decision making are high priorities in Danish cultural life. Through committee structures, local communities have far more involvement in managing services for children than in the UK. It is these committees that are charged with approving and regulating both childminding and centre-based day care for children under 3. For 3- to 6-year-olds there are kindergartens within most localities as part of neighbourhood network systems. Most of them have extensive outdoor playground areas available for the children to play in throughout the day. There are also 'forest kindergartens' to which parents may take their children. In these centres the children spend most of the day – winter and summer – playing in the forests supported by a good adult:child ratio of 1:6 for 3- to 6-year-olds. Many kindergartens are open from 7 a.m. to 5 p.m. Children benefit from a 'coordinated school start' with staff from the two years of a feeder kindergarten liaising with those from Grades 1 and 2 of the primary school. Significantly the workers in the kindergartens are called 'pedagogues' but the approach to promoting children's learning is predominantly through play. The basic training of the pedagogues takes three and a half years.

Peter Moss (1992: 33–4) praised the high quality of provision in Denmark: 'Denmark is in every respect exceptional . . . is the only EC country where publicly funded provision accounts for most of the children in this age group (0–6) who attend some form of early childhood service'. With these kinds of values underpinning provision of services, it is no surprise that early childhood practitioners from the UK who visit Denmark's pre-school settings come back gasping with surprise at the quality of the provision they see – the purpose-built centres, high standards of resources, advantageous staffing ratios. Above all it seems to be the calm informality and physical freedom of the young Danish children, particularly in the forest kindergartens, that is the most striking feature of their daily lives in nursery settings for visitors from the UK.

In France, as in the UK, there is a division of responsibility between the Ministry of Social Security and Health (for day care services for children under 3) and the *écoles maternelles*, under the auspices of the Ministry of Education. *Écoles maternelles* provide nurseries or kindergartens for 3- to 6-year-olds, although increasingly children enter at 2. Almost 90 per cent of children up to the age of 6 benefit from some form of private or public nursery education in France, though there are regional variations in provision.

The aims for nursery education are couched in 'social equity' terms. Goutard (in David 1993: 40) translates these as:

- the prevention of impaired development and early detection of handicaps;
- compensation for cultural disadvantage;
- equalizing educational opportunities.

Already we can sense how the value systems implicit in French cultural expectations result in a fundamentally different way of conceptualizing nursery education. Although there is a 'social rescue' element within the broad aims and the word *maternelle* implies an essential element of nurture in the settings, the *raison d'être* of nursery education is essentially about the word *école*, bringing all children up to appropriate standards for starting school. There are broad objectives for the curriculum in the *écoles maternelles*:

- to turn children into pupils;
- to socialize;
- to promote learning and allow time for practice (Goutard in David 1993: 40).

The curriculum is defined within four broad areas of experience: physical activities, communication activities (including oral and written expression), artistic and aesthetic activities and scientific and technological activities. However, early years specialists are aware, as in the UK, of the downward pressure from schools to focus on preparation for success in academic achievements.

The French Education Act of 1989 divided public, elementary education into three phases: the *pré-apprentissages* (the pre-learning cycle) for children aged 2 to 4 in nurseries; the *apprentissages fondamentaux* (the basic or fundamental cycle) for 5-year-olds in the nursery and 6- and 7-year-olds in school; and the *apprentissages d'approfondissement* (the period of consolidation) for children aged 7 to 11. *Écoles maternelles* staff are now trained in university institutes with those intending to teach throughout the school system in France. Care assistants are employed to work alongside teachers.

In some areas, parents have formed their own *crèches parentales* for children under 3. Parents have to agree to work with the children for some part of each week (perhaps only half a day) and to participate in managing the settings. Unlike playgroups in the UK, full-time staff are also employed under the same conditions of service as early years workers in public or private day care settings. However, most working parents in France still opt for traditional day care facilities for their very young children.

So, as in the UK, the historical events, political imperatives and cultural attitudes within other countries are carried forward into the way services for young children and their families are conceived, established, resourced and managed (Dahlberg *et al.* 1999). For a discussion of European perspectives on early childhood services see David (1993, 1998). For Scandinavian perspectives see Cohen and Hagen (1997).

 ## The historical/sociocultural influences on services for children

One way of conceptualizing how services for children reflect the wider, social context is to draw on Bronfenbrenner's (1979) seminal ecological model of human development for understanding how young children are situated as learners by the societies in which they live. Bronfenbrenner argued that too little attention has been paid to 'the person's behaviour in more than one setting' or 'the way in which relations between settings can affect what happens within them' or 'the recognition that environmental events and conditions outside any immediate setting containing the person can have a profound influence on behaviour and development within that setting' (p. 18). He also argued that the developing person is an *active* agent in the environment, 'a growing dynamic entity that progressively moves into and restructures the milieu in which it resides' (p. 21) and that 'the interaction between a person and environment is viewed as two-directional, that is characterised by *reciprocity'* (p. 22, emphasis added).

Bronfenbrenner's model defines a complex hierarchy of systems in which individual interactions between people are nested. The *micro-system* is the immediate setting in which a child may be at any one time. That setting or environment will be characterized by particular activities and objects (physical features) and people will be assuming particular roles there. So, as we have seen, a child in a day care setting is likely to be absorbed into different kinds of roles from those he or she will encounter in a nursery class. The next level is the *meso-system* and it consists of the networks or relationships between the settings in which a child finds itself at a particular point in her or his development. The networks between home and the child's playgroup experiences or between the child's parents, childminder and private nursery school arrangements are examples of meso-systems. The *exo-system* is the level in which the meso-systems are nested but which does not involve the developing person as an active participant. The exo-system would include the community in which particular children's services are developed and, for example, patterns of employment. So, as we will see in the next chapter, there are likely to be variations in the evolution of services from local authority to local authority because of the characteristics of their particular communities and patterns of employment. Finally, the *macro-system* is the overall cultural/political/social/historical setting in which the other systems are nested. So, we can see how complex and multifaceted the environmental influences upon young children really are. Figure 1.1 presents a version of the Bronfenbrenner model in diagrammatic form.

In Figure 1.1 pre-school education and day care are shown as distinct micro-systems containing the interactions between parents/children and staff. However, there is increasing political/policy pressure for systems to be integrated into one all-encompassing service on one site for children and their families. In Chapter 2 we will discuss the distinctiveness of the services as they now operate, their respective strengths and weaknesses and the possibilities for generating new models of educare as, in line with government policy, we work towards the integration of pre-school education and care. In ten years time the micro-systems now labelled pre-school and day care settings may have very different labels and provide radically different services for children and their families.

   Suggested reading

For a general discussion of key issues in the field of early years education and care in the UK a good starting point is the second edition of *Contemporary Issues in the Early Years: Working Collaboratively for Children*, edited by Gillian Pugh,

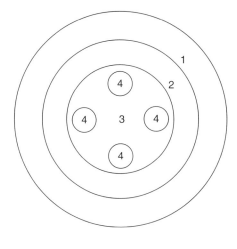

4 Micro-system: for example, the playgroup, nursery class, day care or childminder setting where the child experiences a particular pattern of activities, roles and interpersonal relationships.

3 Meso-system: interrelations between two or more settings in which the child actively participates – for example, home and nursery, childminder and playgroup.

2 Exo-system: settings that do not involve the child as an active participant but in which events occur that affect, or are affected by, what happens in the micro-systems – for example, local authority systems or inspection structures.

1 Macro-system: historical/social/ cultural/ecological environments at national policy level.

Figure 1.1 Historical/cultural influences on services for the developing child

published by Paul Chapman in association with the National Children's Bureau in 1996. Dahlberg, Moss and Pence's book *Beyond Quality in Early Childhood Education and Care: Postmodern Perspectives* published by Falmer Press in 1999 looks at the values underpinning early childhood services, in particular in Sweden, Reggio Emilio in Italy, Canada and the UK.

Goldschmied and Jackson's (1994) *People Under Three*, published by Routledge is a substantial text focused on very young children in group day care, though Peter Elfer and Dorothy Selleck's book, published by the National Children's Bureau (1999) promises to be a useful addition to literature in the field.

Two books, *Working with the Under-Threes: Training and Professional Development* and *Working with the Under-Threes: Responding to Children's Needs* are collections of articles edited by Lesley Abbott and Helen Moylett (1997) on a range of issues in educare published by Open University Press.

For a closer look at assessment and record keeping in early childhood settings see Drummond, M.J. (1993) *Assessing Children's Learning* (London: David Fulton). Cathy Nutbrown's (1998) article 'Early assessment – examining the baselines in early years' (*An International Journal of Research and Development*, 19 (1) (Autumn): 50–62) gives a useful overview of the impact of baseline assessment in early childhood settings and questions the usefulness of current systems.

⓶ Integration of early childhood services

◯ From disintegration towards integration

In contrast to other countries such as Denmark and France, there has been no coherent policy on the provision of early childhood services during the last 25 years in the UK. France has publicly-funded nursery places for 95 per cent of 3- and 4-year-old children and 20 per cent of children under 3. In Denmark, policies for early years services are based on the premise that the care and education of children as part of their preparation to be effective citizens is the responsibility of the whole of society. The UK compares unfavourably to almost all other European countries in its publicly-funded services for young children (Ball 1994; Pugh 1996b). Provision is patchy and services fragmented. Local authorities with a tradition of providing both day care and nursery education (e.g. many inner-London boroughs and large metropolitan areas) have struggled to improve services on limited budgets, but in other areas (e.g. shire counties and outer-London boroughs) parents have limited access to good-quality services. A survey of provision in the UK at the time of the Children Act (1989) would have identified the following patterns:

Nursery education in the maintained sector was mainly half-day (in reality a couple of hours), in order to double the places offered to local children in nursery classes attached to primary schools. Attendance was free. Alternatively, parents paid for their children to attend a few sessions a week at a local playgroup or private nursery school. If they could afford to do so parents might opt to place their children during school hours in a nursery class attached to an independent fee-paying school. Neither half-time nursery education in the maintained sector, nor sessional play group attendance matched the needs of working parents. Full-time nursery education was available in maintained nursery schools, but many local authorities closed them down, on cost rather than quality criteria, as the number of nursery classes in primary schools grew.

Local authority *day care* had become stigmatized as provision for needy or deprived families. The majority of parents who were working still placed their children with relatives or friends, but increasingly – as more women worked – with childminders or in independent nurseries, some of which claimed 'school', others 'day care' status. Where they could afford to do so, some parents employed nannies or au pairs to look after children in their own homes. A review of *parents' preferences* for services, published in 1996 by the National Children's Bureau, concluded that they wanted more provision in general, a focus on the educational and social development of their children in pre-school settings, reliable standards, low costs, accessibility, better information and provision which fitted the needs of their families (Elfer and McQuail 1995). In 1997 the National Foundation for Educational Research reported on a project designed to investigate parents' views of pre-schools (Sharp and Davis 1997a, 1997b). In selecting a pre-school the 953 parents of 3- and 4-year-olds they questioned prioritized its reputation and the happiness of their children rather than the practicalities of nearness to home, hours of opening and cost – though these were of concern to parents. They also prioritized caring staff, good facilities and good security. Just under half were concerned about the teaching of reading and mathematics in the setting. However, parents differed in their priorities according to their child's age, gender, and type of setting they had actually chosen.

A scattering of employers set up work-based day nurseries, especially in settings where women formed a significant proportion of their employees or where shift work was the pattern of employment (for example, in hospitals or telephone-based businesses).

In each of these different day care settings, staff (almost all women) were employed with different conditions of service, rates of pay and training opportunities. In all the settings the status of work in early childhood services was perceived to be low, pay was poor and often staff turnover high.

The fragmented nature of provision for young children in the UK was further exacerbated by the separate structural systems with responsibility for monitoring and managing them. Social services were responsible for all forms of day care provision and for children cared for in 'non-school' settings. In 1989 the Children Act (DoH 1991) legislated for quality control through annual inspections of all day care and voluntary and independent systems offering care for young children. Local authorities were required to carry out a major review of their provision every three years. The tone was of concern to ensure the quality of provision for children 'in need' rather than for all young children, though the intent was to legislate for all.

Meanwhile, control over nursery education had effectively been devolved to school level by the implementation of local management of schools legislation within the educational reforms of the 1980s. The Conservative government's policy was to shift power from local authorities to individual institutions. As local education authorities were restructured to reflect the devolving of budgets and decision making to school level, advisers with responsibility for early childhood education became thin on the ground and relatively powerless to implement coherent local authority nursery education initiatives.

The Conservative government espoused an ideology of market forces determining patterns of provision. The buzz words were 'diversity' and 'choice'. They argued that they wanted schools to be freed from state – but more especially local authority – control. They wanted to devolve the 'purchasing' power for resources, services and staffing to schools themselves. This meant that the head teachers and staff of primary schools were encouraged to perceive themselves as competing with neighbouring schools for custom. Competitiveness between schools was seen as 'a good thing' to lever up 'standards'. An influential right-wing group, the Hillgate Group, argued:

> Their [schools] survival should depend on their ability to satisfy their customers. And their principal customers are parents, who should therefore be free to place their custom where they wish, in order that educational institutions should be shaped, controlled and nourished by demand . . . Schools will have to work to stay in business, and the worse their results, the more likely they will be to go to the wall.
>
> (Hillgate Group 1986: 7, 16)

In response to such pressure, primary schools produced glossy brochures to attract 'custom'. Nursery education within the school where their children would enter statutory schooling was an additional selling point to consumers/ parents. Where it was possible, head teachers cajoled local authorities into cobbling together nursery provision to attract parents to enrol children in their schools. In response to parental demand, head teachers took 4-year-olds into reception classes for full day education, often, as we reported in Chapter 1, with inappropriate space, resources and staffing. Nursery classes were then left to cope with populations of 3-year-olds who required a very different approach to pre-school education. For teachers in nursery classes without formal training in dealing with very young children this was problematic. Many nursery nurses, who had been trained to work with 3-year-olds, struggled to maintain good working relationships in this new climate, sometimes uncomfortably aware that what the teachers were offering the children was inappropriately 'too formal too soon'.

Many nursery and reception class teachers felt alienated and isolated by the climate in their schools created by the educational ideologies and policies of the 1980s and 1990s. Schools focused their energies on their 7- and 11-year-olds gaining good results in SATs for the league tables, and on working towards the 'grand performances' they orchestrated for the dreaded Ofsted inspections legislated for under the 1992 Schools Act. Ofsted inspections, scheduled in four-year cycles, provided the quality assurance mechanism for education paralleling the Children Act inspections of social services settings. However, their focus, even for the inspection of provision for under-5s in schools, was on children's achievements on National Curriculum or *Desirable Outcomes* criteria. They were very different from the kind of inspections carried out by social services personnel on day care settings. School inspections were coordinated by a national body (Ofsted), while non-school settings were inspected by local officers, some based in early years services, some in social services departments and some in independent inspection units established within local authorities.

Even in the early 1980s misgivings were being expressed about the effects of these disparate administrative and accountability systems on access to education and care for the under-5s. A report by Bradley (1982) argued that services for children and families should be better coordinated by establishing clear links between the various agencies, while accepting that they remain distinct. In 1988 the Early Childhood Unit published the results of a survey of systems of provision for young children in all local authorities. Despite interest among local authorities in working towards coordinating services, they reported that 'in the face of low resourcing, seemingly intractable problems over vested interests between departments, and often no clear sense of direction as to the best way forward' (Pugh 1988: 81) little progress was being made in putting their ideas into practice.

However, some authorities did set up pioneering family centres during the 1980s and 1990s where attempts were made to model coordinated services for young children and their families. An early account of the complexity of trying to combine the traditions and cultures of social services-based day care and education-based school systems and ways of working is given in Ferri *et al.* (1981). Well-known examples of family centres that thrived despite the difficulties are Hillfields Nursery Centre in Coventry (the first to be established) and the now internationally-known Penn Green Nursery Centre in Corby. The centres offer flexible hours of day care and pre-school education and, for example, access to health care services for children all under one roof. The term 'educarers' was coined for the professionals who combined care and education in their responsibilities for children. The centres have a strong tradition of actively involving the local community, especially the parents of attending children, in their daily working.

In Strathclyde, the largest education authority in Scotland, a small number of existing pre-school nurseries and day care settings were converted into 'community nurseries' offering flexible services for 0- to 5-year-olds. In Scotland there is a much broader approach to inspecting pre-school education services for 'quality' and the Strathclyde local authority invested strategically both in the evaluation of its initiatives to coordinate services and in the professional development of the staff responsible for implementing change. Nevertheless, as the thorough and informative evaluation reports of the innovation show, attempts to combine the working conditions and lives of teachers and carers in one setting were still problematic (Wilkinson 1994).

In the 1990s the discourse about services shifted from talk of coordination to talk of integration. Pugh and McQuail (1995), based at the National Children's Bureau, produced a short publication to support a more integrated approach to the planning and management of services for young children. They reported on a small-scale study of 11 local authorities where services were categorized as integrated, coordinated or collaborative. *Integrated services* were defined as unified under-5s services with a committee or sub-committee of the council with considerable delegated authority to develop the initiative of integration. *Coordinated services* were in authorities where there were significant formal arrangements between departments at member and officer level. *Collaborative services* were where there were few formal arrangements beyond the ordinary corporate management procedures of the authority. Pugh and McQuail argued that each of the local authorities studied were at a different point – determined by their political, geographical and historical circumstances – on the continuum of integration to collaboration. The authors argued persuasively that 'if the aim is for universal services offering care and education to all children whose parents want it, then an "integrated" approach appears to be most effective' (p. 16). They referenced a report by Lowndes and Riley (1994) on integrated services in four named authorities for the Local Government Management Board which concluded on an upbeat note:

> For the authorities we looked at, it was still early days in terms of evaluating achievements. However, we found a great deal of consensus on criteria for success. Amongst potential benefits for users, improvements in access, choice and flexibility were highlighted, alongside the main goal of maximising development and learning opportunities for young children.
>
> For staff, the potential gains were seen in terms of broader staff development and training (including better use of resources), and the opportunity to deliver a high quality, broad-spectrum service.
>
> For councillors and the council in general, a co-ordinated children's service offered the chance to put key values into practice and to develop higher profile and more proactive, community-based services.

Despite the difficulties inherent in bringing staff together from previously distinct services, the authorities we looked at reported significant achievements in terms of team building and improved access and information for users.

(Quoted in Pugh and McQuail 1995: 8)

The National Children's Bureau also commissioned an economist to estimate the costs of a comprehensive system of day care and pre-school education and to suggest ways it might be funded (Holtermann 1992, 1995). Holtermann's analysis indicated that the costs of such provision – estimated at £2.7 million – would be offset by the savings gained from women coming off benefits to work and additional income generated from their employment through income tax and national insurance contributions. In the end, as Pugh (1996b: 4) pointed out in her cogent argument for improvements in services for young children, in this extract referring specifically to pre-school education: 'universal early childhood education could be afforded, but it would mean either an increased education budget overall (recommended by the National Commission on Education 1993) or a shift within the education budget from higher education to early years (as the Royal Society of Arts report (Ball 1994) argued) . . . the issue is not one of funding, but of priorities and lack of political will'.

The three local authorities with whom we worked were all well along the continuum towards integration of their services; but it is important to recognize that they were operating within the macro-level national policies and imperatives outlined above. During the period of the project, the Labour government required local education authorities to establish 'early years forums' on which independent/private nursery operators, playgroup leaders, voluntary sector interests, childminders and pre-school education providers were all to be represented. These forums were to form the basis of Early Years Partnerships. The partnerships were required to draw up Early Years Development Plans. Constituents were to work in cooperation rather than in competition with each other.

Given the climate of competition fostered over 20 years by the previous government's ideology, symbolized above all in the short-lived voucher scheme described in Chapter 1, this was a sea change in approach. Large and unwieldy committees grappled with the complex task of auditing needs and constructing Early Years Development Plans. Meanwhile, in a residual spirit of promoting competitiveness, the Department for Education and Employment invited all local authorities to bid for 'centres of excellence' that would provide models of good practice in integrated services in their own regions for dissemination to other professionals. By 1999 sixteen centres of excellence, spread strategically across the country, had been funded.

In 1997, an Audit Commission report, *Counting to Five*, warned that many local authorities were struggling to comply with both the spirit and the practices of the new regulations on the education and care of young children. Particularly where local authorities had extensive services already, the voices of independent providers frequently were unheeded in forum debates. Only about half the authorities had formal systems for consultation with the private and voluntary sectors. As 4-year-olds entered reception classes, and council-run nursery classes opened in primary schools, playgroups, perhaps only half a mile from the schools, were forced to close as their numbers dwindled. The Audit Commission report also pointed out that the few nursery schools that did survive cost on average 50 per cent more than nursery classes in primary schools to run; but there was little evidence of authorities 'making better use of these facilities by expanding nursery schools' role' (Audit Commission 1997: 29). The report cited evidence of many vacant or underused places in the reception and nursery classes of schools. Though the take-up of day nurseries' places was reported to be healthy at 90 per cent, the report pointed out that ensuring children's regular attendance was problematic. Consequently poor attendance at day nurseries was identified as a 'value for money' issue.

How did the three local authorities with which we worked for the project fit into this national, macro-level context? If we return to Figure 1.1 on page 17 we are reminded that the working lives of each group of workers who came to the project were influenced both by the macro-system of national policy and practice, but also by the links within the meso-systems developed within local authorities to cope with new legislation and government demands. In order to give a flavour of the local contexts in which the project members were working, a brief account of the main features of each of the three authority approaches to services for under-5s is given below. In each authority strong leadership – both from elected members of local authorities management structures and from officers appointed to head up the reorganization of services towards more integrated systems – was the key to achievement. These were roller coaster years – exhilarating and terrifying by turns – for those with leadership roles in early childhood. You had to hang on tight to the sides in order to survive.

    ## The three local authorities' approaches to services for under-5s

Authority 1

A young children's service was established in 1994. It is located within the education department but within its own building in the centre of the city. Within the building, space is allocated to other organizations such as the Children's Information Service (for anyone concerned with 0–10-year-olds), the Out of School Network, Homestart and the Pre-School Learning Alliance. A training suite and crèche facilities are relocated in other buildings due to service expansion. A multicultural under-5s service with a staff of over 20 is housed in a city-centre school. The team is deployed across ten nursery units working with children between 2+ and 5. The service also has a team with special needs responsibilities to support ethnic minority children with special educational needs and their families. There is a head of young children's services and managers with responsibility for planning and performance, quality and development and registration and inspection. Between them they manage teams of staff with responsibility for planning, external funding, special needs, business links, childminding and educare projects. There is a policy of working closely with business interests in the city in developing services for children. The authority's young children's sub-committee was a sub-committee of the education committee but is now a joint committee with Social Services representation, called the children and families committee.

In its early days the young children's service was led by a head of services with a strong commitment to integration, but in 1996 she reported to the young children's sub-committee:

> The problem for the young children's services has been that the quality not only varies across the city in terms of the individual experience of children but there has been no agreement about how quality is achieved across sectors, nor across professional expertise. This situation has been further complicated by the sometimes fiercely-held beliefs that one system or type of provision is better than another.

She believed strongly in a democratic approach to managing change. The model of decision making adopted involved consultation across groups within 23 local planning areas across the city. Their vision statement and consensus on an approach to maintaining quality across and within all services was developed through a comprehensive programme (September 1995 to July 1996) of discussion and consultation at these local levels. From key principles established by this extensive consultation exercise, a further series of discussion groups were set up to design a quality Kitemark self-evaluation pack. A document called *Starting Together* summarized key principles and procedures for the city services for young children.

Provision in the city includes some young children centres (originally day nurseries) and nursery schools as well as the usual range of nursery classes, playgroups, independent nurseries and childminding facilities. The authority has a government recognized centre of excellence.

Authority 2

A comprehensive nursery education development plan (1987–97) was produced by the city council nursery committee in 1987. The document included an audit of current provision of nursery education in the city. In the plan there was a clear statement of commitment by the council to making nursery education available to all 3- and 4-year-olds by providing all primary schools with nursery classes and enhancing the physical and educational features of existing nurseries. The three nursery schools in the authority were to be phased out as alternative provision was made in local primary schools.

In 1989 an under-8s unit was established to service the newly created nursery and under-8s committee replacing the nursery committee and to meet the needs of expanding non-school based services in the city. The unit was sited in the 'neutral' territory of the civic hall to coordinate the authority's triennial reviews of provision under the requirements of the Children Act of 1989 and to manage and monitor services for young children.

In 1992 the education authority funded a city-wide enquiry into the education of 4-year-olds in primary schools and produced guidelines, backed up by investment in in-service training for existing Reception class teachers of 4-year-olds and in initial teacher training, through an articled teacher training scheme, targeted at training graduates to work with under-5s.

In 1994 the under-8s service conducted a comprehensive city-wide analysis of the needs of families with young children. A quality care and education project was initiated. Representatives from all sectors of provision – schools, playgroups, day care and independent settings – worked together to produce a detailed self-evaluation instrument, *Let's Get It Right*, for group settings catering for young children. Versions were published later for those working with children in out of school settings and in their own homes.

The city has a strong tradition of support for families and children. The Early Education Support Agency was set up in 1987 to run groups for parents and their under-5s where parents take an active part in running the activities. Additionally, widespread support is available to families and children with special educational needs and in 1996 the city began a consultation exercise with 4000 parents of children with special educational needs to elicit their views on appropriate provision.

Early years advisory staff within the education sector of the authority's services were responsible for devising a baseline assessment system which other local authorities bought into when baseline assessment was made compulsory for all children starting school in September 1998.

In 1998, when the government decreed that education should take the lead in the new Early Years Partnerships, the under-8s service was moved from the civic hall into the building housing the city's education departments. In the midst of these physical upheavals a coordinator offering strong leadership worked with the under-8s service, the education department, Social Services and other council departments to oversee the production of the authority's Early Years Development Plan. The council's remit to their officers is to forge interdepartmental collaboration between those with responsibility for education, social services, training, community and benefit rights and housing. As with all Early Years Partnerships, in 1998, the committee, while attempting to come to terms with the daunting partnership brief to coordinate arrangements for education across the disparate strands of provision was faced with a new government initiative under the National Childcare Strategy and required to start work on an Early Years and Childcare Plan.

Provision in the city includes 37 early years centres, 150 nursery classes, and places for 4-year-olds in 244 reception classes, as well as 234 playgroups, 42 privately registered independent nursery schools and day care nurseries, over 1400 registered childminders and rapidly expanding wrap-around care for children before and after school. The authority has an extensive menu of training opportunities to meet the needs of workers in the field, and one of the centres of excellence.

Authority 3

The early years service in this local authority was established by the council in 1993 to provide an integrated framework for the management and corporate development of young children's services across the district. Again it enjoyed strong leadership from the coordinator of the service. The broad aims of the service are to increase the quantity, quality, affordability and accessibility of early years services and to ensure that services respond to the needs of young children and families for care, education and play. The service works in the same building as, and is under the auspices of, the education department.

A partnership with the day care trust paid for the development of a neighbourhood early literacy project called Bright Sparks which was followed by a family literacy programme as part of a successful bid for SRB (Single Regeneration Budget) funding.

The service had also set up strong links with a university to offer training to early years workers, and a comprehensive array of qualifications offering a 'ladder of opportunity' through National Vocational Qualification (NVQ) routes and into diploma and degree programmes. The link between early learning and parent support, education, training and work opportunities was a strong element in the development of services in the authority. Cross-sector training had been provided since 1994, subsidized for childminders, playgroup and mother and toddler club workers, and coordinated through a multi-agency training strategy group. Training for parents had been successfully funded through European Social Fund short basic courses from which participants moved to a range of other opportunities.

Provision in the authority included four nursery schools, nursery classes attached to 68 schools, reception classes in 136 schools, 98 playgroups, 110 parent/toddler groups, 59 private day nurseries and two private nursery schools, 550 childminders, five early years service-run educare centres with subsidized places for low-income families and five social services-run family centres with free places for children in need.

In 1997 the service set up pilot early years units in seven primary schools. The units were designed to offer flexible programmes of education within school hours and settings, but with regular access to outdoor play areas and a 'nursery' style curriculum, to children up to the age of 5. The development of early years units began during the 'voucher' experiment and reflected previous work in the authority to improve provision for 4-year-olds in schools. The units are linked to other services families may require such as playgroups, day care, childminders, out of school and holiday play schemes and parent support and education initiatives. There are now 20 early years units in primary schools in the authority.

The early years service has managed the out of school initiative since its inception in 1993–4. A partnership of two local authorities bid to the Training and Enterprise Council for the contract. The service therefore has a strong involvement with child care 0–14. A children's participation project, working with 4–11-year-olds in out of school clubs has grown out of a partnership with Save the Children. A strong emphasis on children's rights has been a feature of development of the services, and the authority also has a centre of excellence.

Characteristics of the local authorities' services

Although there were differences, common characteristics of the three authorities' approaches to integration were that they developed strategies for reviewing the quality of services which were 'owned' by elected members of committees, officers charged with managing new initiatives and to some extent the early years workers whose practices were to be monitored. They had extensive programmes of staff development at a range of levels for all categories of workers in early years settings. They had tried to gear their 'vision statements' to local contexts and priorities. They had set up structures to manage the budgets which would deploy resources to settings at point of need. However, they had all had to grapple with difficult relationships with key players in other sectors at various times during the period of change. Confronting professional jealousies and often fiercely defended vested interests was perhaps the most difficult part of managing change for the three heads of services and for the early years partnerships across the country.

The effectiveness of types of provision for under-5s: research evidence

Before we are introduced in Chapter 3 to the characters who worked with us on the project, it is important to stand back from policy/practice issues and ask some hard-edged questions about research evidence we have of the *effectiveness* of various forms of early childhood provision. As the head of services in Authority 1 pointed out there are fiercely-held beliefs that one system or type of provision is better than another. But what research evidence is there to substantiate such beliefs?

Trying to tease out the significance of the research evidence we have on the effects of pre-school experiences on young children's development is complex. In the first instance, we have to try to disentangle evidence about the effects on children of attendance at *types of settings* from evidence about the effects of the *quality of experiences* they had in those settings – for example, what kind of curriculum they experienced or the way in which adults behaved towards them while they were there. A third important feature of early childhood experiences away from home is the *involvement of parents* and the impact of continuities or discontinuities of adult/child relationships and behaviours in the two different areas of the children's daily lives.

Finally, as we have seen in the discussion of policy/practice in the UK in Chapters 1 and 2, many young children experience several types of settings. For example, a child may have experience of a childminder, some playgroup sessions and then half days in a nursery class before he or she starts school. So we have to take all these variables into account when trying to determine which experiences resulted in which effect on a child. It is difficult then to ascribe clear-cut cause and effect answers to the questions we asked about the effects of pre-school experiences. However, we do have some research evidence. We will briefly review relevant research below. The 'Suggested reading' section at the end of the chapter should be of assistance to those wishing to pursue the 'effectiveness' arguments.

Types of settings

Osborn and Milbank's large-scale, longitudinal child health and education study (1987) of a cohort of 8400 children in the UK has already been referenced in Chapter 1 (see page 12). Measures used to track the children's progress included their academic attainments (in reading and mathematics) and social adjustment to school (their behaviour) at 5 and 10 years of age. The research team reported marked differences in ability, behaviour and attainment at school between those who had attended pre-school and those who had not. Moreover, they were able to identify that the type of pre-school experienced by children correlated with achievement and behaviour outcomes at 5 and 10.

Children who had attended small, home-based or community-based playgroups and nursery schools achieved the best *academic results* overall. Children who had attended nursery classes or day care or who had simply stayed at home with their parents achieved less well. However, we have already identified in Chapter 1 that a high proportion of the children in day care settings in the sample came from families with social or emotional problems. Thus, although the researchers attempted to control for the characteristics of children in each of the setting samples using 19 social indicators (such as family income) when interpreting their data, we still have to interpret these results with caution. Common sense tells us that children attending small home-based playgroups, for example, are likely to be predominantly 'middle class'. Likewise, because access to remaining nursery schools is often dependent on car ownership, this is likely to indicate that the families taking children to those schools have a particular socioeconomic profile.

The child health and education study also revealed that children who had attended day care settings showed a higher incidence of *behaviour problems* in school (Osborn and Milbank 1987). More evidence came from a study by McGuire and Richman (1986) who found that children attending day care centres run by social services had ten times more behavioural problems than children who had attended playgroups in the same local authority; but again, a closer analysis of the data indicates that the children from a day care background came from families with multiple problems.

Hutt *et al.*'s (1989) project (based at Keele) analysed the effects of attendance on 49 children who had attended four types of nursery provision (nursery schools, nursery classes, playgroups and day nurseries), and found that children with nursery experience showed only slight differences at school entry in measures based on monitoring their attention spans and their relative ability to elicit adults' attention – both key features of 'school readiness'. The most significant difference was that children (especially boys) with nursery experience made more verbal bids for attention than children straight from home and that these verbal bids gained them more adult attention. The differences between the groups became less apparent as all the children were socialized into the bidding routines of orderly school behaviour. This makes disappointing reading for nursery staff who believe that they 'make a difference' to children's start to school. However, we know that teachers make their minds up quite quickly about the 'ability' of young children in their classes, so any behaviour which marked a child out as more 'enquiring' or 'school ready' is likely to result in that child being assigned more challenging tasks or being placed in 'higher-level ability' groups for teaching. Thus the cumulative effect of teacher typifications of children at the start of school can have immediate effects on their likely progress and unwittingly, in preparing children to engage confidently with adults in institutional settings, nursery staff may indeed affect children's achievements at the beginnings of formal schooling.

Research into the effects of attendance at day care settings has tended to focus on measures of emotional adjustment (see Sylva and Wiltshire 1993), probably because of residual anxiety about the effects of 'maternal deprivation' which had been so influential in Bowlby's work in the 1950s (Bowlby 1953). Bowlby argued that all children are biologically programmed to form an attachment to a primary carer. His studies of children in residential care indicated that children who had not enjoyed this attachment were unable to form lasting and meaningful relationships in later life. Later research indicated that it was the quality of care, rather than the effect of care *per se*, that could have damaging effects on children's emotional adjustment.

Quality of experiences

In terms of the effectiveness of pre-school provision there has been confusion in the literature between the effects of settings and of the curriculum models and the quality of experiences to which children have been exposed in those settings.

The most frequently quoted research in the field of the effectiveness of pre-school curriculum is the report on the long-term gains for children in the United States of America (USA) who were exposed to the High/Scope Curriculum in the Perry Pre-school Project. The High/Scope Curriculum is characterized by: high quality, active learning experiences for children; a 'plan-do-review' sequence in the way children are encouraged to work supported by adult interactions; an adult/child ratio of 1:8; and close involvement of parents in the programme. Every parent of children involved in the pre-school programme had frequent visits from trained workers to ensure that there was consistency between the learning experiences offered within the programme and what parents did with the children at home. A longitudinal study showed that children who had experienced the programme were more likely to achieve academically in school. More significantly, long-term monitoring of the children showed that as they grew up they had greater self-esteem, more realistic vocational plans and were prouder of what they had achieved. In adulthood they were less likely to be involved in crime, unemployment, teenage pregnancies or drug/alcohol abuse (Schweinhart and Weikart 1993). (For a detailed account of studies of the effectiveness of pre-school in the USA see Sylva 1994.)

In the USA there is research evidence about the effects of high- and low-quality day care on children. Howes (1988) studied 87 children, half of whom had been enrolled in high- and half in low-quality settings. High quality was defined as settings where the child interacted with a few primary caregivers in any one day, the turnover of staff was low, staff were well trained in child development and there were generous adult:child ratios (1:3 for 0–12 months, 1:4 for 1–3 years, 1:8–12 for 4–6 years). Low quality was the reverse of these indicators. Family background information such as mother and partner's patterns of work and child care arrangements were collected by questionnaires to the parents. When the children were 8-years-old their teachers and parents were asked to respond to questionnaires focusing on their academic work and behaviour both in school and at home. The study showed that there was a relationship between children's achievements and emotional adjustment and the stability of the day care arrangements they had experienced as babies and toddlers. Children who had fewer changes in care arrangements were more likely to achieve good results at school than those who had experienced many changes. Another important American study found a relationship between the working conditions of the staff who cared for children in 227 day nurseries in five cities, and the quality of care provided for the children (Whitebrook *et al.* 1989). Where working conditions for staff were good, the quality of care for the children was higher.

In the UK, a longitudinal study based at the Thomas Coram Research Unit of day care arrangements for the first child of 255 families in London tracked their development up to the age of 6 by visiting them at home on four occasions (Melhuish 1991). The children were tested on language development and intelligence. They were observed both at home and in care settings. Questionnaires were completed by their mother, carers and teachers. Information was collected about the mother and her partners' work patterns and reasons for choices and changes in child care arrangements. As with the Howes (1988) study, the results showed that children who experienced more changes in day care arrangements had a slower rate of cognitive development during their first three years. However, the children who had been in day care settings showed no more signs of problem behaviour than those who had been cared for at home.

A research and development project, 'Effective Early Learning' (EEL), led by Pascal and Bertram (Pascal *et al.* 1997) at Worcester College of

Higher Education, has focused since 1993 on improving the quality of children's learning in all types of early childhood settings. The EEL framework 'Framework for Quality' is organized around ten dimensions of quality. Key foci of quality are embedded in a scale which measures children's involvement in learning episodes and a scale which measures the engagement of adults in children's learning.

In all these studies, the most important outcomes for children's long-term success in both education and social relationships are associated with whether their pre-school experiences left them with feelings of high or low self-esteem. This important concept will be explored in detail in Chapter 4, where we will explore the relationship between young children's sense of 'self' and their developing attitudes or 'dispositions' to learning.

 Integration of services for young children in the future

So research evidence does give us some insights into the effectiveness and/or appropriateness of both the types of provision and the quality of experiences for young children before they start school. In summary:

- the most effective forms of provision demonstrate close, working partnerships between parents and staff in the settings;
- parents have clear views on the need to expand provision for young children and to match that provision to the changing needs of families and patterns of employment;
- the most crucial features of high quality in any pre-school setting are the expertise and commitment of the staff;
- children who attend some form of pre-school provision achieve higher in conventional aspects of education – for example, in English and mathematics;
- in particular children from disadvantaged backgrounds achieve better results in school if they have had experience of nursery education or good-quality day care.

Simply integrating services will not necessarily enhance the quality of provision for young children and their families, though in terms of equity it must make sense to even out the benefits of flexible services and ensure that they are accessible to as many families as possible (Makins 1997). What really would make a difference is a profound change in attitude in this country to the provision of services for children so that, as in Scandinavian systems, it is taken for granted that society will value them and divert funding to them. Such changes will only come about through the ambassadorship of the professionals working both at policy and practice levels in the field of early childhood. It is to their professionalism that we turn in Chapter 3.

 Suggested reading

An accessible book on research evidence about the quality and effects of day care, with references to studies in a number of countries, is Hennessy, E., Martin, S., Moss, P. and Melhuish, E. (1992) *Children and Day Care: Lessons from Research* (London: Paul Chapman Publishing).

Osborn and Milbank's (1987) report on the longitudinal child health and education study in England, Wales and Scotland, *The Effects of Early Education* (Oxford: Oxford University Press), is currently the most comprehensive account of the long-term effects on children's later performance in school.

In 1997 funding was allocated by the Department for Education and Employment for a research project to investigate the relationship between pre-school experiences and achievement in school. The project, 'Effective Provision of Pre-School Education' (EPPE project) is directed by Professor K. Sylva and promises to give us significant information about the effectiveness of different types of pre-school experiences. Readers should watch for publications associated with the research.

Moss, P. and Penn, H. (1996) *Transforming Nursery Education* (London: Paul Chapman Publishing) offers a strong critique of existing services in the UK and a vision of how they might be in the future.

③ The inquiring professional

◯ The importance of adults

The research on early education we outlined in Chapter 2 and the work on children's learning and development we discuss in Chapter 4 all point to just how important the quality of adult-child interactions and the context of those interactions are, if children are to be helped to see themselves as people who can and do learn easily.

When we planned the project on which this book is based we therefore focused on how the project would support pre-school practitioners as they in turn supported children as learners. We knew that the project had to deal with a number of challenges to professional practice already discussed in the previous chapters. In summary they were:

- the diverse nature of pre-school provision and the professional groups which contribute to provision, which between them draw on the professional cultures of health care, nursery nursing, social work, voluntary work and education;
- an emphasis on children's entitlement to educational provision which pre-school practitioners were obliged to meet;
- pre-school practitioners had to meet this entitlement while they were themselves developing new professional identities as both educators and carers.

While we planned the project we worked with three aims which we hoped would meet these challenges. The aims were ambitious and we were aware that our project could only be one small part of a much wider set of efforts aimed at creating an informed *community of practice* of educarers. The three aims were:

1 the development of a new form of professional practice which drew on the best of current traditions of education and care;
2 the professional development of educare professionals;
3 some useful contributions to the knowledge base that informs the professional development of practice and practitioners.

These aims were particularly ambitious because the project started just as pre-school practitioners were beginning to get to grips with the curricular demands of an emphasis on the educational purposes of pre-school provision. Consequently the project itself became the vehicle through which practitioners met these new demands in their settings and developed some of the ideas that were to underpin their professional practices.

We were working with frameworks drawn from sociocultural psychology which drew our attention to the meanings given to the language and the materials used by practitioners. In the project we were hoping to observe the development of common understandings when, for example, early literacy and numeracy were discussed, and to see an increased capacity to recognize the educational potential in familiar materials. We were particularly interested in focusing on how high-quality interactions between children and educarers helped children to learn to enjoy learning.

The ideas on children's learning, early literacy and early mathematics used by practitioners in the project are outlined in Chapters 4 to 8 in this book. In this chapter we shall look at the wider project and its use of case study and action research; the individual action research projects of the practitioners; and the importance of evidence-based practice for the development of early years professional practice. Our major focus, therefore, will be practitioner research, how to do it and how it can support the development of practitioners and practice.

   ## The wider project

The project is outlined as three action steps in Figure 3.1. Steps 1 and 2 each lasted four months and Step 3 took ten months. In meeting the three aims we outlined in the previous section we focused on the three action steps. However, we also gathered additional information through interviews, repertory grid techniques and questionnaires. Data from these have informed the direction of the project and ultimately our own evaluations of the initiative.

Step 1 consisted of a series of workshops where we led sessions on children as learners in literacy and in mathematics, action research and parental involvement. In Step 2 participants built up case studies of current practice on specific areas of provision in their own settings. In Step 3 they undertook action research curriculum and staff development projects with their colleagues in their settings. In both Steps 2 and 3

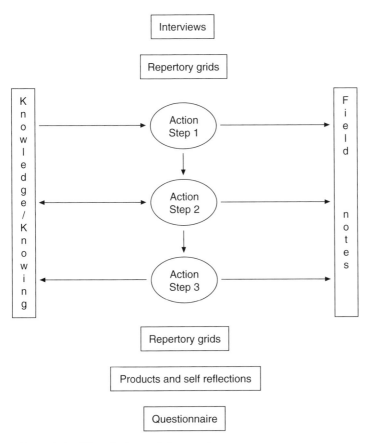

Figure 3.1 The design of the project

regular workshops were held to exchange information across settings and we visited each setting to give whatever help was needed.

The participants were originally 20 pre-school practitioners from three local authorities, four local authority senior managers and the authors. The practitioners came from a range of professional backgrounds and settings. Backgrounds included teaching, social work and nursery nursing. Settings included day care, nursery schools, local authority special initiatives, childminding and a work-based nursery at a local hospital. The practitioners' names (pseudonyms) and individual project focuses are shown in Table 3.1 (four practitioners left the project because of moves or competing priorities). The practitioners were selected by their local authorities because of their ability to work with other professionals in order to share the outcomes of the initiative once it was completed. All three local authorities were therefore thinking carefully about how the benefits of the project could be sustained after its 18-month life.

Table 3.1   The key practitioners and their projects

Practitioner	Project	Age range
Alison	Mathematics	(18–60 months)
Amy	Mathematics	(0–18 months)
Bernie	Mathematics	(36–60 months)
Frances	Music: literacy and mathematics	(18–36 months)
Gill	Mathematics	(0–36 months)
Ivy	Literacy	(0–18 months)
Jade	Mathematics	(36–60 months)
Jenny	Literacy	(0–18 months)
Josie	Mathematics	(18–60 months)
June	Mathematics	(0–18 months)
Meg	Literacy	(18–36 months)
Melissa	Mathematics	(36–60 months)
Millie	Mathematics	(0–18 months)
Molly	Literacy	(36–60 months)
Reza	Mathematics	(0–18 months)
Val	Literacy	(18–36 months)

The initial concerns and interests of the practitioners in the areas of literacy and numeracy were elicited through a short open-ended questionnaire given at a workshop at the start of Step 1 (at this stage in the project we used the narrower term 'numeracy' to reflect government policy). The responses were placed in six categories: concern about their own personal knowledge/information about literacy and numeracy; resource and curriculum concerns; staff development needs; issues relating to home/school relationships; assessment/recording/reporting worries; issues about children's learning of literacy and numeracy in their settings. The number of people mentioning each of these issues is shown in Tables 3.2 and 3.3.

Their written responses revealed that there were some differences between concerns about coping with numeracy and with literacy. Participants appeared more confident in the area of literacy, how it was resourced and how parents might provide support. However, they did feel that they needed help with understanding the developmental sequences that underpin young children's acquisition of competence in literacy. Numeracy appeared to be relatively unexplored territory and this was particularly the case in relation to working with parents. The detailed responses also revealed the breadth of concerns which included catering with different age groups, bilingual children and the gendering of early education. Underlying these concerns was a sense that an emphasis on specific learning outcomes at the end of the pre-school experience might lead to the Key Stage 1 curriculum being filtered down to pre-schools.

Table 3.2 Main concerns about literacy (number of respondents for whom an issue was a concern is given in bold)

Knowledge/ information	Resources/curriculum	Staff development needs	Parents (home/ school)	Assessment/recording/ reporting	Children's learning
1 Approaches to teaching reading (6)	1 Appropriate resources (7)	1 Learning to value home literacy (1)	1 How to involve parents actively (8)	1 Assessment strategies (2)	1 Responding to bilingualism (3)
2 Developmental sequences of literacy learning (4)	2 Funding of resources (2)	1 Lack of teaching experience (1)	2 Raising parents' awareness of the value of family literacy (6)	2 Diagnosing/ responding to 'failing' children (1)	2 Preparation for school literacy (2)
3 Cross-cultural approaches to literacy, mark-making (1)	2 Range and appropriateness of activities (2)	1 How to develop quality one-to-one interactions with children (1)	3 Encouraging parents to have positive attitudes to libraries etc. (1)		3 Encouraging boys to like books (1)
3 Desirable outcomes for literacy (1)	3 Book lending programmes (1)		3 Supporting parents' own literacy needs (1)		3 Responding to needs of mixed age groups (1)
	3 Suitable books for babies (1)		3 Environmental settings and reading (1)		3 Targeting 0–12-month babies (1)

Table 3.3 Main concerns about numeracy (number of respondents for whom an issue was a concern is given in bold)

Knowledge/ information	Resources/curriculum	Staff development needs	Parents (home/ school)	Assessment/recording/ reporting	Children's learning
1 Developmental sequences in maths learning (5)	1 Lack of suitable resources (6)	1 'Teaching' numeracy (8)	1 Low levels of numeracy in community (1)	1 Strategies for diagnosing children's learning needs (2)	1 Quality of learning experiences in maths (3)
2 Desirable outcomes for numeracy (3)	2 Structured play/ quality activities (2)	2 Staff personal confidence in maths (3)	1 Informing parental expectations (1)	2 Baseline assessment (1)	1 Preparation for school maths (3)
3 National Curriculum (2)	2 Narrow approaches to numeracy (e.g. just counting) (2)	3 Vocabulary of maths (1)	1 Involving parents (1)	2 Diagnosing/ catering for 'failing' children (1)	1 Involving children with English as a second language in mathematical learning (3)
4 Cultural differences in key concepts (1)	3 Lack of time given to numeracy (1)	3 Response to inspection criteria (1)			2 Catering for needs in mixed age groups (2)
		3 Building support networks (1)			3 Gender issues (1)

If this were to happen, it was feared that it would erode a number of firmly held professional beliefs about what constituted appropriate learning environments for very young children.

All the project participants were, therefore, united in the professional belief that if educare were to form the basis of pre-school practice it had to be developed from the pockets of sound practice and expertise to be found among those already working with very young children. It was hoped, therefore that a strong sense of what educare could be would develop through a sound mixing of the best of all the pre-school cultures found among the participants, helpfully flavoured by some research-based contributions from the authors. The blending of the mixture to create an understanding of educare depended entirely on the activities and contributions of the individual practitioners and it is to these that we now turn.

Step 1: the workshops and readings

The contribution of the authors was most evident at Step 1. We ran workshops on literacy, numeracy, doing practitioner research and working with parents. We also produced digests of relevant research which were given to all the participants to help generate ideas for the individual projects that were to occur in the next two steps. Step 1 was also important as an opportunity to share current concerns and interpretations of those concerns, to visit each others' settings and to get a feel for where everyone was coming from as a practitioner. The trust, openness and shared meanings that were built up slowly over the four months of Step 1 were, we would suggest, crucial to the success of the project.

Step 2: the case studies

In Step 2 the practitioners undertook small case studies in their own workplaces. We suggested case study as a starting point for the research for four reasons:

1 case study as a form of audit or analysis of current provision is an essential starting point for action research;
2 case study allows you to look at a complex aspect of practice or provision in a highly focused way;
3 small-scale case study is a manageable way of becoming familiar with methods of collecting data;
4 the material gathered in the case studies could be used as the starting point for discussions between participants at our monthly workshop sessions, allowing good ideas to be shared across settings.

So what is a case? We worked with social science understandings of case and case study. Here a case is usually described as a 'unit of analysis'. It can be, for example, a family, a work team, an area of the nursery, a child, an aspect of the curriculum. Cases are therefore seen to consist of sets of complex relationships that can be observed within a fairly distinct boundary. Yet, at the same time, cases also interact with the context in which they are situated so the boundaries are permeable.

You will remember from our discussion of Bronfenbrenner's (1979) work in Chapter 1 that we were able to understand 'the child as learner' by locating her or him in relation to his or her family, the social policies that influenced the patterns of family life and the political priorities which led to those social policies. Cases therefore provide distinct focuses for us as researchers, but can also be connected to events outside the case. In our project the cases were aspects of the curriculum, specific areas in the nursery settings or sets of relationships between parents and professionals. These cases were located within the efforts of local pre-school providers to get to grips in 1997 with the curricular and professional development demands of *Desirable Outcomes* (DfEE/SCAA 1996a).

Cases can be used in a number of ways in research (see Stake 1994 or Edwards and Talbot 1999 for further details). In Step 2 of our project we wanted cases to be descriptions of what was going on so that they could be used as stimuli for discussions between the key practitioners and also between them and their immediate colleagues when the time came for planning Step 3. We also knew that once professionals start to look in a focused way at aspects of their own provision they see them afresh and any number of professional issues arise when thinking about what has been seen. Our research partners therefore started their case studies wanting to answer the question *what is going on here?*

The case study process

Each participant was advised to go through the following process:

- think about the provision in your setting;
- look at your development plan if you have one;
- identify one area where you feel strongly that provision could be improved;
- identify the precise aspect of provision on which you want to focus;
- negotiate with colleagues in the area you have identified to allow them to feel comfortable about being part of the case study;
- select the data collection method(s) you will need in order to find out what is happening;
- plan when you will be able to collect the data without disturbing the case;
- Gather your data.

Gathering case study data

To ensure that the data that were gathered did give a valid picture of provision we asked practitioners to design their case studies so that they used three methods of data collection and collected their data systematically over a period of time. In doing so we were working with the idea of *triangulation* which is central to robust case study work. Triangulation, as the term implies, means getting as strong a purchase on the case as is possible by approaching it from a number of angles. 'Strong' and 'as is possible' are important concepts in practitioner case study. Case studies do rely on rich data, but there comes a point where the over-zealous practitioner researcher can disrupt the case in the quest for evidence. We strongly advised practitioners to do only what was feasible. We were therefore keen to work with data collection methods that were fairly unobtrusive.

Research diaries were kept by everyone in the project. These were spiral bound hardback notebooks. They were used in the following way. Working from the front we used the left-hand pages to jot down observations of, for example, children at work in the construction area or notes made during or immediately after staff meetings or workshops, and we dated the notes. If the books were not at hand jottings were made on the paper that was available and later clipped into the notebooks. The facing right-hand pages were left free to be used for immediate reflections on the notes or for later reflections once themes started to emerge or when someone at a workshop said something which helped to interpret what had been recorded. Working from the back of the notebooks we collected useful addresses, clipped in cuttings from professional journals or the press, or wrote references to books or papers we heard about in our discussions. The diaries then served as records of observations and developing interpretations of events and proved to be the most useful research tool for everyone concerned.

Photographs were used to produce time sequence observations. If a sense of an activity over a period of time was needed, for example to see how children made use of the materials available in an area of the nursery, then photographs were taken at regular time intervals of, for example, one every 60 seconds for ten minutes, to produce a time sequence of ten photographs. These proved to be very useful case study data for our purposes as the pictures provided the opportunity for considerable discussion both at workshops and in the settings between the practitioners there.

Video recordings can be particularly useful when trying to capture the detail of interactions or how children use particular resources, but are not always as useful as one might expect when trying to capture the more general flow of activities across a busy nursery setting. Ivy, who worked with mothers to help them interact with their babies, gathered some very useful data using a video camera which allowed her to capture the gradual thawing of the mothers as they learnt to play with their children.

Written observations were made using a range of methods:

- narrative descriptions of key events were written and stored in the research diaries;
- specific observations of children using materials in settings were undertaken using the schedule we discuss in Chapter 8;
- the target child method of observation developed by Kathy Sylva and her team was used to track specific children or to observe how staff were interacting with children.

The target child method of observation (Sylva *et al.* 1980) is so useful and flexible that we shall describe it here (it can also be found in Edwards and Talbot 1999). The method as we used it in the case studies involved the following stages.

1 Identify a target to observe – for example, the target could be a child or a colleague – and select the setting for the observation – for example, the child in the water area.
2 Identify the time you will observe the target (you will need at least 15 minutes for a ten-minute observation and you should undertake more than one ten-minute observation of the target, though not necessarily on the same day).
3 Prepare a set of observation schedules. These consist of sheets of A4 paper each divided horizontally into five blocks and vertically into first a narrow column, followed by two columns of equal width (see Figure 3.2). One sheet of paper is used for five minutes of observation. When you use it you will write the time in the first column – for example, 10.01 against the first block, 10.02 against the second etc. In each block in the second column you will write down everything that you see your target doing or saying in the course of one minute. You will keep the third column blank to be used for annotating your observations later. For ten minutes of observation you will need two sheets.
4 Find a place to observe where, if possible, you can hear as well as see your target.
5 Write down as quickly as possible what your target does. You will need an easy to read watch so that you know when to move on to the next minute block on the observation sheet. You will also need a shorthand system such as initials for names and arrows for actions.
6 After ten minutes, stop and take your observations to somewhere where you can have five minutes to tidy them so that they will make

Time	Observation	Comment/Analysis
10.01		
10.02		
10.03		

Figure 3.2   Part of a target observation schedule

sense later. Use the reverse sides of the observation sheets to make any notes you wish about the event. For example, you might want to note what the colleague had said she had hoped to achieve, or why you were observing that particular child.

7 Repeat your observation at least once with the same target person in the same setting.

8 What you put in the third column will depend on the focus of your study. If, for example, you are interested in children's mark-making as Mollie was, then you will focus on what adult actions led to successful mark-making or to a child refusing to cooperate and you will begin to label them in the third column.

Notes from staff meetings proved to be extremely useful. A number of participants started their data collection with 'brainstorms' with colleagues in which they listed, for example, how joining in the musical activities in the nursery was already benefiting all the children, or what strengths parents had as educators of the children in their nursery. Sometimes these notes provided very useful diagnostic material for planning just how fast or carefully it would be appropriate to work with colleagues at Step 3. Melissa, for example, through staff meeting discussions, was able to clarify her understanding of the extent to which her co-workers saw the educational potential in the number activities she was making available for children.

Other written material such as booklets for parents, curriculum plans or assessments of children were easily collected. Their relevance and currency was discussed at workshops and notes were made of the discussions in the research diaries.

Tape-recordings can be very helpful when focusing on children's language or interactions between children and adults. However, the noise levels in most nurseries and the speed at which most young children move around meant that it was not always an attractive option. When tape-recordings of children's talk were successfully undertaken they were specifically set up by taking children to a quiet corner and recording them while they worked at an activity. Staff meetings were sometimes recorded, but it was often difficult to hear everyone and the recordings had to be listened to, which was time consuming.

Questionnaires and interviews can also be used in case studies. However we did not use them very much in our project, partly because they too can be very time consuming, are difficult to do well (particularly when researching your own setting) and produce a lot of data that take a long time to analyse. However, Meg drew usefully on information from a short questionnaire to parents about how much they wanted to be involved with her centre to gauge the pace at which she should work with parents. Reza and June used both interviews and questionnaires in their attempt to discover how much music was part of the lives and language development of the children in the multicultural nursery in which June worked. We did not recommend interviews as they can be intrusive and disrupt the case. However, if you would like to know more about interviews and questionnaires see Oppenheim (1992) or Edwards and Talbot (1999).

We found that short written observations, photographs and short written records of conversations made during observations to be the most useful pieces of evidence both in our discussions at workshops and when practitioners discussed what they had noticed with their immediate colleagues. This was because the written evidence could be photocopied and read and the photographs looked at by a group of people.

These observations therefore became public texts around which the expertise of everyone involved could be shared and developed. Insights from education colleagues about the educational potential in activities were useful to those with a care background, while those who worked in care settings drew on their understandings of attention to children's emotional state and the quality of adult-child interactions and contributed these. We were aiming at developing a community of educare practice in which meanings were shared and knowledge about how children could be supported as learners was constructed. The case study discussions based on evidence from such a variety of settings were fertile starting points.

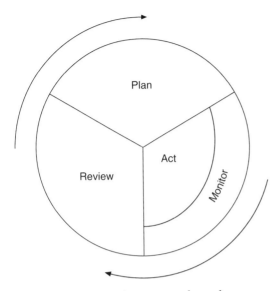

Figure 3.3 An action research cycle

Step 3: the action research

Step 3 was the action research stage of the project. In this stage particip-ants developed an aspect of practice in their settings, monitored the development and looked at its impact on the experiences of children. Importantly, they took the ideas that had been developed among the group in Steps 1 and 2 back into their own settings and integrated them into practice while helping their colleagues work with them too.

We used a simple model of action research which started with *review* and moved on to *planning,* which was then followed by *action.* The action was carefully *monitored* and then *reviewed* along with possibilities for further development which would enable the cycle to start again (see Figure 3.3).

Our case studies in Step 2 were our reviews. Conversations in the workshops and in the various pre-school settings about the case study data were the jumping-off points for planning the actions to be taken in Step 3. The conversations focused on how the situation described by the cases could be developed to bring out the educational potential in the activities. Ideas were shared and plans for curriculum development began to take shape. We were ready to plan our actions. At that point we had to get very practical and think about *feasibility* and *timescale.* There is always the danger that practitioner researchers can become so excited about the possibilities for development found in a case study that they try to do too much too quickly.

Using timelines for planning

To deal with feasibility and timescale we used timelines to guide our planning. These proved to be very important because they constantly reminded us of just how long change takes and how much care needs to be put into developing the confidence of colleagues as they work with new ideas. An outline timeline for planning the development of children's mark-making is shown in Figure 3.4.

In Figure 3.4 we see that four months between September and December were taken up with preparing for the involvement of everyone in trying out the new ideas in practice. The action occurred between January and April and time was set aside throughout that period for staff to regularly discuss the developments as they were occurring. The outcome was a set of curricular guidelines on mark-making that everyone had some part in producing.

The phases in this example were as follows:

1 discussing the case study findings with colleagues and introducing the ideas developed in conversations in Steps 1 and 2;
2 planning any changes to nursery organization and noting resource needs;
3 ordering resources;
4 making changes to the area where mark-making will occur;
5 trying out the ideas in a small way and monitoring the trial;
6 evaluating the trial of the new ideas;
7 adjusting ideas and replanning;
8 agreeing how the actions will be monitored;
9 undertaking actions and monitoring the actions;
10 timetabling regular meetings to discuss what is being learnt about new strategies and the children;
11 adjusting strategies if necessary;
12 final evaluation and the development of curricular guidelines on mark-making.

Finding time to talk

In the project we used action research with two aims in mind. First we needed a way of allowing the expertise that existed among all the practitioners involved to be made explicit so that it could be shared and contribute to the knowledge base of educare. The knowledge that underpins expert practice is often referred to as tacit knowledge because it has become so much a part of the actions of expert practitioners that they simply don't need to think or talk about it. By asking practitioners to plan, monitor and evaluate aspects of practice, and to do that while drawing on some of the ideas we had shared about learning and curriculum,

Figure 3.4 A Timeline for a piece of action research on mark-making in the construction area we were asking them to be explicit about their practice and, as they talked, to contribute their own meanings and interpretations to the developing discourse of educare. Our second action research aim was that the systematic and public analysis of strategies to promote children's learning would mean that we could have some confidence in the reliability of the grounded curricular guidance the local authorities had been promised as an outcome of the project.

The need to talk about practice meant that our action research plans emphasized the opportunities for discussion within each setting, and between settings when the participants discussed progress at our monthly workshops. The need to undertake systematic analysis of actions meant that colleagues needed to work, as they did in the case studies, with non-intrusive but robust methods of data collection. Also, because we wanted to evaluate the effect of new ways of working, it was important that they collected evidence about what the children were able to do as a result of these innovations.

Monitoring the action

We used the same data collection methods that were suggested for case studies at Step 2 and found the diaries particularly useful as records of the story of each development. We added to these methods by attending particularly to collecting (i) examples of what the children did and (ii) feedback from parents. Evidence of what the children did included photographs of completed models or games; photographs showing how children were using resources – for example, measuring the boats they built out of big blocks or holding and enjoying books; their attempts at mark-making and emergent writing; and written observations which included their use of language and materials.

Feedback from parents was collected in two ways. Comments made by parents about their children and their new experiences were noted immediately in research diaries by almost everyone. For example, Millie and Amy noted the following comments about their songbook.

> I felt silly at first. But when I saw how Sarah responded I began to enjoy our singing sessions.
> I realize how OK it is to hold Joseph and sing to him. We both love these times together.

However, we also found that a great deal of evidence came from materials that were passed between pre-school settings and homes. The distressed mothers in Ivy's project were helped to build up brief profiles of their children and record their successes in interacting with them in games and songs at home. The mothers of the toddlers in Val's project made books which contained their child's photograph and information on what the child was doing which passed between the parents and Val. In both of these examples the books came to mean a great deal to the parents but also provided Ivy and Val with important evidence of the success of their projects. The parents in Josie's project on mathematics at home and in the nursery were eager to provide evidence of their children's work with number at home with, for example, photographs of children jumping down steps and counting them or proudly showing their sets of five nail varnishes laid out on a bed.

The evidence that was gathered during the monitoring of the planned actions was used, like the case study data, as shared texts and the basis of conversations about practice. We will see in Chapter 8 how staff in Alison's centre all used the same format for their observations of children as they worked as beginning mathematicians in the construction area and discussed what they observed at weekly meetings in ways that both shared what they had noticed about children and what they had learned about practice.

What we learnt from action research

What we learnt about how to support children as they experience mathematics and literacy-based activities in pre-school settings will be outlined in the next five chapters. At this point we shall focus on what the participants reported that they had learnt about themselves as practitioners and about the practice of educare at the end of Step 3. First of all we shall look at their final reflections on their own experiences in the project at the end of Step 3 and then we shall draw on elements of a questionnaire completed four months after the project ended.

We asked each of the practitioners to write up their personal reflections on their experience of the project. In summary, action research seemed to serve a number of purposes. For Jenny it appeared to be a lifeline which kept her going while working alone on her project with babies and books, while at the same time it fired her intellectual curiosity and helped her focus on the principles that lay behind the project. For Meg in her project on parental involvement in literacy and for Jade in her work with parents and everyday mathematics, the commitment to the project and the support of the group sustained them when other pressures took over. In Jade's case this included the need to evacuate the centre as a result of flooding which certainly meant adjustments to the timeline! For Melissa, involving colleagues in action research allowed her to start the curriculum developments she thought had long been necessary and allowed her to evaluate and adjust the developments as they were being implemented. For Molly, action research helped her rethink how she could best support the professional development of her staff and how important it was to help them see for themselves what needed to be done. For Alison, the project provided the focus for an energetic and enthusiastic staff team, and for Frances it was the opportunity to try out in a systematic way her own theories about how children gain from being in a musical environment. The common feature in all the reports was how much each of the participants felt they had learnt while trialling their ideas as action research and how much had been gained from being part of a group both at the level of the wider project and in their own settings.

Questionnaire data gathered from open-ended questions in the questionnaire distributed four months after the end of Step 3 revealed, for example, how much more aware colleagues were of the strengths that children bring with them to their pre-school settings and how they could use the particular strengths of parents to help their children develop as learners. The questionnaire data, in summary, revealed an increased confidence in being able to work flexibly and interactively with children as learners. This broad analysis is supported by the evidence gathered using repertory grids which we shall discuss in the next section.

Earlier in our discussion of action research we identified two aims for the action research phase of the project. These were (i) to help make explicit the tacit expertise of the participating practitioners so that it could be shared and contribute to the knowledge base of educare and (ii) the systematic analysis in practice of the curricular guidance we were jointly developing. Our aims were very much in line with those suggested by John Elliott for action research. Writing about action research and teachers he suggests:

> Teachers may be unaware of their actions and of the beliefs and assumptions (theories) that underpin them. Understanding comes through the analysis of evidence about practice and the generation of new knowledge via the formulation and testing of action hypotheses in the light of such analyses.
>
> (Elliott 1994: 137)

Action research is clearly a powerful way of generating and evaluating the practical knowledge of educare. We also agree with Elliott's claim (Elliott 1994: 137) that action research can bring together 'the processes of pedagogical transformation and theory generation'. Our practitioner partners transformed aspects of their own practices at the same time as developing the practical knowledge of educare. We would, however, stress that the practical knowledge that was produced is itself contestable. That is, the practical knowledge of educare should be consistently scrutinized by a well-informed profession and not become ritualized in empty practices. Therefore at the core of any notion of educare should be the idea of the educare professional as an informed and sceptical practitioner.

Developing informed confidence through research into practice

The project required practitioners to make important changes in their practices in order to provide the children with their educational entitlements and to research those changes so that they could share their experiences with other practitioners. The practitioners who were involved clearly felt it was a worthwhile experience. But we also had other evidence.

The research design provided in Figure 3.1 shows that we started the project by interviewing participants. We chose our interview sample of six participants to enable us to get views about current and future provision from experienced practitioners from the range of backgrounds and settings that was found across the project. We then used the material we gathered in the interviews to structure a more detailed data-gathering exercise using repertory grids. Repertory grid methodology is a sound and efficient way of finding out how people make sense of their immediate world (for further reading on repertory grids see Fransella and Bannister 1977 or Fransella and Thomas 1988).

We used a grid that would enable us to find out how participants were feeling and thinking in eight specific situations such as doing a puzzle with a child or talking to an inspector. Having decided on the situations we then used our interview material to provide us with statements about how practitioners might be making sense of each situation. These statements are called *constructs* in repertory grid methodology. Constructs are often likened to the blinkers through which we make sense of our experiences. For example, when we meet something new to us we categorize it using constructs. Constructs are bipolar, which means that a construct is a dimension with opposite feelings at each end. If whether people are gentle or aggressive is important to us we will place people we meet somewhere on the construct 'gentle-aggressive'. So when we meet someone new we might use a construct that has gentle and aggressive as its two poles to judge the extent to which the newcomer is gentle or aggressive. Our constructs are also personal and based on our own previous experiences, so gentle-aggressive may not be a construct used by everyone. Indeed, others may be judging the same newcomer as either aggressive or a wimp and hoping that she or he is aggressive.

We therefore had to be careful to select constructs that would make sense to most of the participants, that would help us measure the changes we wanted to measure and could be used when thinking about how as a professional one might think and feel in a particular situation. In Table 3.4 you can see the constructs that were finally selected and in Table 3.5 we have listed the situations.

Table 3.4 Rankings of importance of constructs before and after undertaking research

	At the start of Step 1		At the end of Step 3	
	Average rating	Rank	Average rating	Rank
Feel confident about what you say/think there may be important gaps in what you are saying	3.7	1	4.6	1
Feel confident that your colleagues would say the same/have doubts that your colleagues would say the same	3.1	5	3.9	6
Know exactly what you want a particular child to learn/have quite general learning intentions in mind	3.2	3	4.2	3
Have the resources you need available/lack the resources you need	3.1	5	3.9	6
Think you are getting somewhere/feel frustrated	3.1	5	3.9	6
Think you can focus at the curriculum/have a number of competing concerns	3.0	7	4.0	4
Feel happy about the curriculum emphasis/ feel a sense of loss with the emphasis on the curriculum	3.4	2	4.4	2

Maximum rating = 5
Number of responses at the start of Step 1 = 12
Number of responses at the end of Step 3 = 13

The participants completed the grids individually by being talked into each situation by one of the authors and were then asked whether, for example, they felt confident in what they were saying or thought that there might be gaps in what they were saying. Participants were asked to respond on a five-point rating scale. So if they felt very confident while doing a puzzle they would record a rating of five, or if they felt that there were at least some gaps while talking to an inspector they would record two or three for that situation.

The grids were completed early in Step 1 and at the end of Step 3. We were therefore able to assess the impact of the project on the participants' thoughts and feelings about quite specific aspects of practice. In Table 3.4 we have given average ratings and the ranking for each construct

Table 3.5 Ranking in feelings about situations before and after undertaking research

	At the start of Step 1		At the end of Step 3	
	Average rating	*Rank*	*Average rating*	*Rank*
Doing a puzzle with a 3-year-old who is a quick learner	3.7	1	4.0	6
Water play with a 3-year-old with delayed language development	3.2	5	3.9	7
Explaining to a new colleague how work in your nursery helps children to become literate	3.0	7.5	4.2	3
Explaining to a new colleague how work in your nursery helps a child to become numerate	3.0	7.5	4.2	3
Talking to a parent about how she or he can help her or his 3-year-old to start to read	3.3	3	3.7	8
Planning the literacy curriculum with colleagues	3.3	3	4.2	3
Planning the numeracy curriculum with colleagues	3.1	6	4.1	5
Explaining to an inspector how the environment has been created to support children's learning	3.3	3	4.3	1

Maximum rating = 5
Number of responses at the start of Step 1 = 12
Number of responses at the end of Step 3 = 13

and in Table 3.5 the average ratings and the rankings for each situation in both stages of the project. We selected the constructs so that a high rating would represent professional confidence. But we do recognize that, for example, having competing concerns is not necessarily a professional weakness in the complex world of educare.

In Table 3.4 we see very little difference in the ranking of importance of each construct at the start of Step 1 and the end of Step 3. Indeed there is also very little difference between each rating at the time of assessment. However, there are important differences between the average ratings at the start of Step 1 and the end of Step 3. The average ratings on each construct are considerably higher at the end of Step 3 in each case. We suggest that this increase demonstrates an increase in informed confidence among the participants over the period of the project. More specifically of particular interest in relation to the project aims are:

- satisfaction with the curricular emphases manifested in the project;
- satisfaction with resources suggesting that the educational potential of existing resources was being recognized;
- recognition that colleagues were also learning;
- the outstandingly high rating given to participants' own knowledge base.

When we turn to Table 3.5 we, of course, see a similar increase in average ratings between the start of Step 1 and the end of Step 3, but we also see changes in the rankings related to situations. These changes are important because they tell us where participants felt most informed and confident at the start of the project and again at the end. The pattern shown in Table 3.5 shows us that at the end of the project:

- participants were far more confident about explaining numeracy and literacy to new colleagues and about explaining to an inspector about how the nursery supported children's learning;
- the more traditional aspects of nursery provision (i.e. doing puzzles and talking to parents) showed slight increases in scores but were overtaken by more curriculum-related matters;
- as we might have predicted from our diagnoses shown in Tables 3.2 and 3.3, colleagues were slightly more confident when planning the literacy curriculum than the numeracy curriculum.

These results are exciting because they show that a great deal of learning had occurred and that participants were demonstrating that learning in how they thought about their everyday practices. Our sample is small and the project quite specific but we would suggest that the experience of evidence-based practice we monitored and supported did have a highly positive impact on the professional development of participants.

 Enquiring professionals in educare

We shall discuss the contexts of professional development in Chapter 9. Here we simply start to alert you to what our data told us about the importance of collaborative action research as a way of developing new professional identities. By professional identity we mean *a way of being, seeing and responding* while working professionally. We would expect an educare professional to work responsively and with flexibility and, for example, see the mathematics in a piece of striped material or wrapping paper and help a child to also see some of the mathematics available there.

We were, therefore, particularly excited by the repertory grid data which suggested that our research partners were seeing increased educational potential in existing resources. Our field notes at workshops in Steps 2 and 3 had indicated that colleagues were thinking and acting with increasingly educational insights as they worked with familiar materials. The repertory grid data seemed to confirm these indications and suggested that a new professional culture of educare was being developed in which existing materials were given new meanings as they were being used in new and more informed ways.

These findings are very much in line with work on professional cultures and how participants in a culture learn to use the materials and the language associated with cultural activity in increasingly informed and culturally accepted ways (Lave and Wenger 1991; Cole *et al.* 1997). Professional cultures and sociocultural psychology are complex fields of study, but there are lessons to be learnt from them when considering educare as a new form of professional practice. Much of the work in this field considers how learners are guided into being active members of existing cultures. In our study we were looking at how a new form of professional culture was being developed in action, and sociocultural psychology provided a useful set of lenses through which to observe aspects of the action that took place.

For example, sociocultural psychology helped us to see how a new form of professional culture was taking shape in our project through evidence-based discussions of developing professional practices. James Wertsch, writing about cultural memories, reminds us of the extent to which we build up a sense of ourselves as a community through the language we use when we recall aspects of the community and recount its stories (Wertsch 1997). Action research, with its emphasis on public discussion of the narratives of practice, is illuminated by Wertsch's analysis. In our study, discussions of what was happening in pre-school settings were informed by the research-based knowledge provided by the authors and by the current research of the settings-based participants. These discussions proved to be useful vehicles for professional community building and meaning sharing.

 ## Suggested reading

Helen Penn has edited an international collection of papers which theorize the policy and practice developments in early childhood services entitled *Theory, Policy and Practice in Early Childhood Services* (Buckingham: Open University Press) and is due to be published in 1999. The chapter by Anne Edwards draws on the study discussed here and attempts to answer the question 'Research and practice: is there a dialogue?'

An excellent guide to the practicalities of action research is Hopkins, D. (1993) *A Teachers' Guide to Classroom Research,* 2nd edn (Buckingham: Open University Press). You should not be deterred by the title, as the ideas discussed transfer very easily to pre-school settings.

Action research and case study are also strands in a practical guide to practitioner research which is sensitive to the demands of workplace research: Edwards, A. and Talbot, R. (1999) *The Hardpressed Researcher: A Research Handbook for Education, Health and Social Care* (London: Longman).

4 Young children as learners

○ The what, who and how of learning

Decisions about curricula for young children are often gambles. We simply can't predict exactly what knowledge and kinds of expertise will be needed 20 years from now. However, we can be pretty certain that the very young children of today need to become adults who are able to adapt to work practices that will change throughout their working lives and able to cope with the changing demands coming from families and communities. Those of us who are involved in the education of young children therefore need to focus on helping children to become learners, to enjoy learning and to feel that they are people who are able to learn. This is no small challenge but it is a safe bet that investment in children's dispositions to learn will pay dividends.

Our research partnership was stimulated by the publication of *Desirable Outcomes* (DfEE/SCAA 1996a) which, when we started, represented government policy on the pre-compulsory education phase of provision for children. The emphasis in the document was clearly on the *what* of learning and children's entitlement to sets of experiences which provide opportunities for them to demonstrate the beginnings of competence in specific fields of knowledge which is in turn assessed through baseline assessment (see Chapter 1, page 3).

How different is the emphasis placed by Schweinhart and Weikart (1993: 4) when they discuss the lasting change that occurred as a result of High Scope interventions with disadvantaged children in the USA in the 1970s:

> The essential process connecting early childhood experience to patterns of improved success in school and community seemed to be

the development of habits, traits and dispositions that allowed the child to interact positively with other people and with tasks. This process was based neither on permanently improved intellectual performance nor on academic knowledge.

Schweinhart and Weikart point to dispositions – that is, orientations towards the world around us – which ensure that children approach activities from which they might learn in ways that allow them to be open to the learning opportunities in them. Schweinhart and Weikart's emphasis is on helping children to see themselves as people who can learn. Their focus is on the *who* of learning – that is, on creating learners. An emphasis on disposition is similarly found in the New Zealand early years curriculum (MoE 1993) where they refer to dispositions as 'habits of mind' and 'patterns of learning' which provide the foundation for future independent learning.

Desirable Outcomes (DfEE/SCAA 1996a) also appeared to differ in emphasis from 'The Rumbold Report' on quality in early years provision (DES 1990) despite the report's obvious influence on it. Interestingly in a section entitled 'A curriculum for the under fives' the authors of the 1990 report highlight the following statement: 'the process of education – how children are encouraged to learn – is as important and inseparable from, the content – what they learn. We believe that this principle must underlie all curriculum planning for the under fives' (DES 1990: 9). Here there is an attempt to ensure that the focus on the *how* of learning that has been central to early education is not lost in a mission to ensure that children get their entitlement to particular experiences.

The three emphases just outlined can be summarized as:

1 identifying *what* children are to learn;
2 creating children *who* are learners;
3 attending to *how* children learn and *how* adults support their learning.

There is, however, a danger in selecting just one of these emphases as the basis of practice. Traditionally, early education has been based on a developmental view of how children learn. Important as this is, recent thinking about learning suggests that the *what*, *who* and *how* of learning are crucially interlinked. For example, a disposition to learn in the domain of mathematics is nurtured by previous success with mathematics. This success is, in turn, connected to children's developing capacities to deal with mathematical concepts and the support that adults give them. The early years practitioners in our partnership confirmed this analysis of the interrelatedness of all three aspects of learning by moving rapidly from the recognition of, for example, mark-making as a curriculum area to be covered, to concentrating on creating contexts in which children became mark-makers and where adults supported them.

As the project became increasingly focused on supporting children while they learnt from the experiences provided in the different settings, we began to frame these experiences with a view of learning which allowed us to take into account the *what, who* and *how* of children's learning and helped us to plan future developments. This view is loosely called a sociocultural approach to learners and learning. The approach offers a focus on learners, how they are supported, and the cultural messages in the contexts in which they learn.

A sociocultural view of learning: learning and context

It is so easy when presented with a new label to assume that it stands for something very different from what has gone before. This is not the case here as sociocultural views on learners and learning build on well-established traditions. For example, sociocultural approaches have a lot in common with Piagetian ideas about learning. They acknowledge that learning occurs as a result of active involvement with the environment; and that children construct, that is build up, increasingly complex under-standings over time, so very young children will operate, at times, with misconceptions about the world. Sociocultural approaches are even more clearly rooted in Vygotskian perspectives on learning and therefore emphasize how adults can support children as they learn; how children learn what is important in their culture through interactions with more experienced members of that culture; and how language carries the meanings and values of a particular culture when it is used in that culture. Let us, therefore, look at four of the key features of a sociocultural approach to understanding learning and how we found them useful in the project. The four key features are:

1 the situated nature of learning (i.e. we learn to do what we think the context demands of us);
2 the relationship between our sense of who we are and what we do (i.e. between our identities, dispositions and our actions);
3 an understanding that learning occurs through interaction with others (i.e. through language and imitation);
4 an understanding that learning occurs through interaction with objects (i.e. through using objects in the same way as others do).

Learning is situated

Sociocultural psychology tells us that learning is a process of being able to *participate* increasingly effectively in the world in which we find ourselves.

At birth, that world is fairly straightforward, albeit heavily emotionally charged, consisting of the presence or absence of sources of food and comfort. It soon becomes more complicated so that, for example, young children learn that although rowdy behaviour might be fine in the garden it is not appropriate in the supermarket. By the time children are ready to enter compulsory schooling they should have some idea of how to participate as pupils, rather than members of a family, when at school; and how to begin to think as, for example, mathematicians and historians when given tasks which demand specific approaches.

In summary, action and therefore learning is heavily situated. Learners look for cues in contexts for guidance on how to participate. One challenge for early years professionals has always been how to ensure that children learn all that they can from the experiences provided. So much depends on how children see, interpret and respond to the learning opportunities available to them. As Schweinhart and Weikart (1993) indicate, a disposition to interact positively with people and with tasks seems to be a crucial indicator of long-term success as a learner. A sociocultural perspective on learning goes a little further than simply promoting a positive approach to experiences by suggesting that children's actions need to be within the bounds of what is considered appropriate. So, for example, young learners learn to sit and listen to stories; to use pictures as clues to the meanings of text; that stories have endings; and so on.

Alison's development of the construction area in her centre in order to provide 3- and 4-year-old children with opportunities to participate positively and appropriately with materials, illustrates these ideas in practice. Having resourced the area with books about boats, small- and medium-size wooden blocks, 'engineers'' helmets, tape measures, paper and pencils, staff encouraged children to work in pairs to build boats. Once finished, the boats were measured and the measurements recorded by the children. The children were encouraged to participate – i.e. think and act – as designers and mathematicians and to participate in a process from planning to recording. The children tackled the activities in ways that reflected their own physical and intellectual development and achieved a sense of success through completing the activities. They left the construction area with memories of an experience in which thinking and acting as designers and mathematicians was associated with their own effectiveness.

Identities and dispositions

One way of looking at disposition so that we can become clearer about how adults can support children's dispositions to respond positively and appropriately, is to connect disposition to children's developing sense of who they are and what they can do. To make the connection we need to look briefly at the idea of 'personal identity' – that is, the *who* of learning. Rom Harré, for example, uses the words 'self' and 'identity' interchangeably and talks of both as organizing principles for action (Harré 1983).

Harre's definition helps us to see that our sense of who we are – which will include what we are capable of doing – guides our orientation to the world around us and ultimately how we participate in it. For example, if a child's identity includes a belief that she is good with numbers, she will find herself attracted to number activities. At a more detailed level, if that identity includes a capacity to see mathematics as sets of patterns then the child will seek out the patterns in the learning opportunities provided. In other words, she will have a disposition to engage with aspects of the mathematics available in the experience provided for her.

The children in Alison's construction area were, through their role play, developing dispositions to design and evaluate as part of the construction process. They were able to operate at levels which reflected their capabilities and their successes were supported and recognized by the adults.

Dispositions are rooted in our sense of our likely effectiveness. The challenge for educators is to assist the development of a sense of effectiveness through careful and sensitive support while children acquire the capabilities and understandings which will underpin their effectiveness. Here we connect the *how* and the *what* to the *who* of learning and need to examine the relationships that support early learning.

Learning often occurs in interaction with others

The learning trajectory followed by most children from birth to 5 can be summarized as a gradual and parallel shift from interdependence to independence and from a focus on personal meanings to a focus on public meanings. Hence, the role of carers of young children is to support them as they acquire the capacity to participate in their social worlds. The responsibilities of adults therefore change in relation to the development of children's capacities to cope effectively with the world around them.

These responsibilities shift from the close and often symbiotic (mutually interdependent) relationships of key caregivers with infants immediately after birth and through much of the first year of life, to supporting children as they begin to experience and act upon a world that is external to their relationship with their caregivers. Finally the role becomes one of assisting children to understand the external world in the way that it is understood by other members of society. Let us look at each of these three stages in turn and consider their implications for supporting children as learners. We see these stages of adult support as a continuum and are all too aware that in interaction with children, adults will find themselves moving backwards as well as forwards along it. Although we are labelling the stages we emphasize that the boundaries between them are fuzzy.

The intersubjective phase

Initially children experience the world, and participate in it, through their relationships with their main caregivers who bring them into involvement with some of the basic features of social life by highlighting particular behaviours. The most important of these behaviours is the turn-taking that underpins, for example, language development. Young babies are not, however, entirely passive participants in these relationships.

Colwyn Trevarthen's detailed analyses of videotaped interactions between mothers and babies in their first few months of life (see Trevarthen 1977 for an introduction to his work) has drawn attention to the finely-tuned patterns of interaction that occur and the extent to which these interactions can be mutual and not simply a matter of infants responding to their mothers. Trevarthen describes this turn-taking and synchronizing of responses as *co-regulation* (Trevarthen 1993). Importantly, co-regulation seems to happen as part of interactions in which mothers adapt their behaviour to the rhythms of their children and allow them to appear to be taking the lead so that a conversation-like interaction (or *proto-conversation*) occurs.

The close relationship between infant and caregiver which Trevarthen observed and which enables an infant to experience the world in the physical and emotional safety provided by the relationship is characterized by *intersubjectivity*. Intersubjectivity was first described as the *meshing* that occurs between infant and caregiver which allows an infant to be inducted into understandings of what is important in the caregiver's culture (Newson and Newson 1975). It is often described in studies of infancy as a *meeting of minds*, where one of the minds is already steeped in the culture and where the other is being brought into the culture.

Intersubjectivity therefore demands considerable attention to the emotional state of infants and a capacity to slow down and tune into young children's ways of experiencing the world so that children are brought into interaction with the world. One of the most important elements of intersubjective relationships is how they help infants to develop as members of society with their own intentions and capabilities. A key feature of the adult role in an intersubjective relationship, in the western world, appears to be to act *as if* the infant has intentions and is able to make evaluations. We see this behaviour in the conversations that mothers have with infants about feeding – for example, 'You want your bottle now don't you, I can tell'. This *as if* behaviour appears to prepare the child for her or his later intentional and purposeful interactions with the world.

What we know of intersubjectivity is reason enough, we would argue, for ensuring that key worker systems are safeguarded, particularly for infants. If education is to be a feature of provision from birth we need to attend carefully to the subtle and demanding nature of work with babies. Clearly this is an area of provision where a great deal of settings-based research is essential given the importance of children's relationships with their primary caregivers in their families. In our research partnership understandings of intersubjectivity fed two quite different projects.

Millie and Amy in their inner-city nursery worked cautiously and carefully in this area though the use of 'action songs'. They collected songs from the nursery workers and the parents involved in the nursery. They then produced a song book with, alongside each song, suggestions for ways of holding the babies and for actions associated with the lyrics. The songs were sung both at home and at the nursery. In both settings the infants were held in similar ways and were involved in consistent sets of patterns and responses with both sets of caregivers.

Millie and Amy's work also connected with another important feature of relationships between children and their caregivers in the first year of life: the involvement of children in *language formats* (Bruner 1983). Language formats are usually described as the frequently routine language repetitions associated with, for example, bath or mealtimes, or found in action songs. Bruner argues that these formats help children to understand that conversations involve interactions and that there is order to language. Therefore language formats provide children with important pre-linguistic skills.

Ivy's work with intersubjectivity was, however, quite different and involved her in therapeutic work with distressed parents. She worked in collaboration with speech therapists in her project with mothers who were experiencing problems in interacting with their babies as a result of depression. These mothers and their children quite clearly had not experienced intersubjective meshing and the children were not interacting appropriately with others in the nursery as a result. Ivy role-modelled interactions with the children which involved eye contact, sustained interactions through the language formats of repetition games and ways of responding to the children's overtures such as their smiles, offerings of objects etc. In the informal setting, where Ivy would sit on the floor alongside the older children, mothers were encouraged to watch and to respond when they felt ready to do so. Although attendance was often spasmodic, video evidence shows how mothers learnt to respond to their children and to sustain several turns of interaction with them.

Learning to look outwards

Once infants have gained some sense of their own intentionality – for example, that adults will respond to them – and they are secure in their capacity to engage in various forms of conversational turn-taking, they are ready to begin to look beyond the familiar patterns of meaning making found in their intersubjective relationships. This is an important stage in the move towards being able to deal with the social world and the public meanings that operate within it. Again adults can help or hinder this stage in a child's developmental behaviour.

The key concept here is a *joint involvement episode* (JIE) (Schaffer 1992). In a JIE an adult and a child pay joint attention to, and act together on, an object. An object may be, for example, a toy or part of the environment. As children get older the object may be, for example, a play on words or a joke. The important point is that JIEs direct children's attention to objects and events outside their relationships with their caregivers while giving them opportunities to act on these objects within the security and fund of expertise available in their caregiver relationships.

Schaffer therefore emphasizes the need for adults in JIEs to be sensitive to children's needs and abilities so that children are able to try out their ability to communicate with others while receiving the kind of support that assists them to develop as communicators. There is now considerable evidence to connect experience of JIEs with language development. Gordon Wells, for example, in his study of children's language at home found a strong and positive relationship between the rate of language development at 30 months and the proportion of speech directed by the mother to the child during shared activities such as joint book-reading, play or sharing household chores (Wells 1985).

As we discussed JIEs during our workshops and related them to activities in various pre-school settings we saw them as developmental extensions of the sound meshing that occurred in intersubjective interactions with infants. It was clear, for example, from Ivy's project that JIEs could not occur before the children had experienced the support that came from intersubjective relationships with primary caregivers. During our workshop discussions of evidence from the projects we gave both intersubjective meshing and JIEs the label of 'good one-to-ones' and were particularly excited by the way JIEs provided a framework for understanding the role of adults in interactions around objects with children from their second year of life. Jenny's project with babies and books, which aimed at encouraging mothers to interact with their babies and toddlers as they shared books, illustrates the continuum of 'good one-to-ones' that was a feature of several of the projects.

Working independently (with just a little help)

This phase marks the final stage in the shift to children's independent action and use of public meanings when they communicate with others in the pre-school years. It is frequently the most difficult for adults to manage as it requires them to maintain sensitivity to children's need for support together with an ability to intervene without inhibiting the flow of children's meaning making in context. In the previous two stages, adults have provided a supporting structure for children's actions and meaning making as part of their close relationships with children. Now the support has to increasingly occur outside relationships that have forms of dependency at their core. We therefore need to look carefully at how adults provide support, or *scaffolding*, at this stage of children's development as learners.

Scaffolding has been defined as 'the contingent control of learning' by an adult with a child (Wood 1986). This definition is important because the word 'contingent' reminds us that scaffolding as support needs to be sensitively in response to (that is, contingent upon) the learner's need for assistance. The responsive nature of scaffolding is particularly relevant when working with very young learners who are gaining confidence as effective participants in the world around them and are developing dispositions to engage with the learning opportunities provided.

All too often, when scaffolding is discussed in the context of compulsory schooling and class teaching, it becomes simplified into a format for lesson planning where children are expected to work increasingly independently over the course of a lesson. Scaffolding learning is, however, a much more interactive process and demands close observation and continuous assessment of children as they participate in the learning contexts provided for them. In some ways scaffolding can be seen as a form of *guided participation*. Scaffolding or guided participation is, however not simply based on interactions between adults and children. Children's participation in an activity is also, in part, shaped by the resources available and the expectations for the use of the resources in a particular setting.

The children in Alison's construction area were guided into particular ways of participating as builders with blocks by the selection of materials available to them (for example, the sizes of the blocks available, tape measures, role play clothing and paper for recording); and by staff who brought resources to their attention and encouraged them to plan, complete, measure and record. The following is another example of the kinds of scaffolding interactions that occurred in Alison's construction area. The area this time was designed to engage children in working with shapes and the adult was undertaking a focused observation of the child. (The child was 4 years and 6 months.)

The child (C) takes out a shape book and turns to a page with a house on it. The adult (A) sits down and watches (C).

C: I want to make a house. (*Gets out large wooden bricks. Turns to adult.*) How do I do it Sally?

A: Look in the picture book, there's a triangle box at the top and a square shape for the house with straight lines.

C: (*Picks up two wedge bricks and places them on floor. Glances at the book and points at the top of the house. Places a rectangle brick in front of the two wedges.*) I don't know what comes next Sally.

A: Right, tell me about this so far then.

C: It's the roof.

A: Right. Then we need the long straight lines to make the side of the house.

C: (*Looks at the bricks and selects a long rectangle. Places it at right angles to the roof on the left side and repeats for the right side. Looks at A, and A nods in response.*) Which one?

A: (*Points to the house in the book.*) The small rectangle for the bottom of the house.

C: (*Picks up brick.*) This one?

A: (*Shakes head.*) Look at the shape. Is it the same as this? (*Points at the book.*)

C: No . . . erm . . . what is it then?

A: Well, have a think. Tell me what you think it is.

C: Don't know. (*Looks at the book and then the bricks.*) Is it a square?

A: Yes, that's right, a square.

C: (*Places two rectangles. Sits back on knees to observe the house.*) We need windows and a door. (*Places three square bricks as windows and a rectangle for the door. With A, takes a photograph of the house.*)

There are a number of features of this interaction that illustrate the kind of scaffolding that adults can give children who are to be encouraged into independent thinking and acting:

- the adult's assessment is focusing on what the child can do and she is keen to find out as much as possible though observation and interaction;
- she is not allowing the child to enter a dependency relationship with her;
- she alerts him to other supporting material in the context so that he should be able to work without her presence on a similar task in the future;
- she uses the language of shape and sets up opportunities for the child to do the same;

- she encourages, through her silences, the child's own evaluations of the work;

In summary, the adult is managing to ensure that the child remains in control of the activity and provides support which is tailored to the learning focus of the construction area. She is engaging in what Bruner refers to as the courteous conversations which support learning (Bruner 1996) and which acknowledge the importance of children's own search for meanings as they participate in the world.

Bruner (1996: 57) explains how children are brought conversationally into the meaning making that is shared in their cultures:

> [children's] naive theories are brought into congruence with those of parents and teachers not through imitation, not through didactic instruction, but by discourse, collaboration and negotiation. Knowledge is what is shared within discourse, within a . . . community . . . this model of education is . . . more concerned with interpretation and understanding than with the achievement of factual knowledge or skilled performance.

Bruner's view of how adults support young children as learners was certainly supported by our research partners who were anxious that too much attention to the *what* of learning would mean that they would have to work in what they saw as inappropriately 'teacherly' ways with pre-school children. They frequently pointed out, as we noted in Chapter 2, that they were not teachers and did not want to be.

Their concerns were not surprising given the 'features of good practice' identified in *Desirable Outcomes* (DfEE/SCAA 1996a). These made several references to 'teaching' and the definition of teaching included 'giving clear explanations and appropriate adult intervention' while play and talk became 'media for learning'. If nothing else, these definitions hardly represented the subtlety of Bruner's analysis of how learners are brought into cultural knowledge and develop the capacity to become effective contributors to their cultures. Indeed, like Bruner, we would argue such a view of teaching in the pre-school phase is unlikely to assist children as they develop the dispositions or identities as effective learners that we suggest are essential.

Learning occurs through the manipulation of the tools of a culture

This feature of a sociocultural approach to understanding learners and learning provides a useful framework for looking at resource-based pre-school provision. Cultural tools (Rogoff 1991; Wertsch 1991) include the meanings carried in the language we use – for example, referring to children as 'little' allows them to get away with breaking rules and is a reason for their being sent to bed before their older brothers and sisters. Tools can be intellectual and include the way we think about activities – for example, the children in Alison's centre were encouraged to plan and evaluate. Also, cultural tools are the objects or artefacts with which we surround ourselves and with which we interact in culturally specific ways. For example, although pieces of wooden puzzles make good missiles, we offer them to children as puzzles and expect them to use them as such. Similarly, children are guided into participation in pre-school settings by learning the accepted way of using familiar materials, such as sand or water, while in the nursery. We can bring all three features of cultural tools together when we consider how adults help children work with the materials that are available to them in most pre-school settings.

Every project in our research partnership in some way involved changing the use of existing resources in the various pre-school settings in order to make the most of the educational potential in them. In Molly's nursery the construction corner took mark-making as a focus and children recorded their achievements. Staff in Melissa's High Scope nursery school used 'play people' with the construction materials to support children's use of the language of position – for example 'inside', 'next to' etc. The mothers in Jenny's babies and books project found ways of using books with their children that they had not previously been aware of. In each of these examples the adults used familiar material in ways which exploited their educational focus. Also in each of these examples either Molly, Melissa or Jenny modelled for the other adults how the materials might be used. (We shall discuss staff development in Chapter 9.)

In order for children to understand how material resources are used and learn the ways of thinking associated with them they need to experience those resources in conversation with those who do have some understanding. So when first given a wooden puzzle children need to work on it with someone who will use it as a puzzle and not a missile store. While jointly assembling the puzzle, through trial and error or the sorting of pieces, children learn how members of their knowledge communities tackle such tasks. They learn not only the meanings of words 'here is another blue piece', but also how to approach the task by sorting, planning, testing and completing, and they do this as Bruner (1996: 57) suggests through 'discourse, collaboration and negotiation'.

The role of adults in guiding children into being competent users of the cultural tools of their society is therefore crucial. In our partnership we used research into what children and adults could do in pre-school settings as a way of developing shared understandings across a range of settings of what the adult role can be as children are supported as learners. Above all, we concluded, the adult role is to open gateways to new understandings for children as they participate increasingly knowledgeably in the world around them. Opening gateways demands that adults journey alongside children and are themselves aware of the gateways and the opportunities that lie beyond them.

 ## How children develop as thinkers

What goes on in children's minds is a fascinating field of study but we are probably still only at the 'best bet' stage of creating a complete framework for understanding children's thinking. However, we found that the insights into children as thinkers and learners offered by constructivism (a view that we construct our understandings of the world over time) and by sociocultural psychology, resonated with the experiences which were being recorded in the pre-school settings. We therefore worked selectively within these frameworks as we made sense of the children's experiences we discussed.

In the previous section we explained how children learn through acting on and trying to make sense of the world around them. We also emphasized that they are enabled in their meaning making by the support of sensitive others who are alert to their current ways of seeing, interpreting and responding. In this section we shall look at some of the features of the meaning making process and pay some, but fairly brief, attention to developmental aspects of children's thinking. We shall focus on children as individual and as social thinkers.

Children as individual thinkers

The frameworks offered by Piaget for understanding how children process the information they glean from their experiences fall into the 'best bet' category and underpin most constructivist perspectives on children as learners (see Wood 1988). We shall therefore start with them. The key words are *schema, assimilation, accommodation, equilibration* and *development*. Through these key concepts Piaget's work helps us understand just how learners construct understandings of their worlds.

Schema are the mental structures into which we organize the knowledge we hold about the world. For example, 3-year-old Naomi playing in the water area might think that big things sink and small things float. She will have a sinking/floating schema, which although not in tune with expert knowledge, does work. The schema will change once she experiences enough counter evidence and needs another way of organizing that knowledge to make sense of the world.

Assimilation occurs when we take in information which does not demand that we alter our existing schema. For example, another large object that sinks will not require Naomi to adjust her schema. Assimilation can also occur when we experience something that is so beyond our capacity to understand it that we cannot engage with its full cultural meaning and therefore there is no impact on our schema. In the case of adults, this might be a discussion of time and space in the context of globalization or fine detail of the arguments for and against Britain joining the Euro.

From such examples it should be evident that young children frequently find themselves in situations where they simply don't have the knowledge that would allow them to make sense of an object or experience. We see this when children make 'music' with a keyboard, or mark-make when recording orders in the 'cafe'. We also see it when they turn an object to their own purposes and ride a broom handle or hand out leaves as 'cakes'. Much of children's play is therefore assimilation and it is through this kind of imaginative play that children become familiar with the rituals and objects that are part of their worlds. Play of this kind is also important for adults. For example, many of us approach a new word-processing programme by initially playing with it to see what it can do. But children need a great deal of assimilation-oriented play, as the familiarization with objects and how they might be acted upon is an essential part of meaning making.

Accommodation is what happens when we adjust our existing schema to take in new information. This is often simply a case of refining existing schema so that, for example, a child acknowledges through his language and behaviour that there is a schema that both he and adults call 'hat' and that his shorts do not belong to it. Sometimes the adjustment is quite radical, demanding new schema, such as when Naomi recognizes that some large objects float and some small objects sink. A strictly Piagetian interpretation might argue that Naomi would manage the reorganization of her schema without adult help. A more educationally-oriented interpretation, and one we would advocate, would suggest that the adults' role is to provide the language support that helps the children to label their new understanding. We saw an example of such support earlier in this chapter, in Sally's language when she scaffolded the child's use of the language of shape while in the construction area.

Importantly, accommodation only occurs when the difference between existing schema and the new information is not too great. (Hence the importance of the opportunity for familiarization through imaginative play.) Problem solving play is particularly valuable for encouraging accommodation of new information, as during this kind of play children are able to work using their existing schema on materials that have been selected to give them the opportunity to refine those schema. One should not, therefore, see assimilation and accommodation as distinct phases in a learning cycle which can be planned for. Rather they occur together as a child tests out existing understandings and has to adjust them to be able to cope with new information. The meaning-making process can, in this way, be seen as a search for a balance between what is understood and what is experienced.

Equilibration is the term used by Piaget to explain the constant adjustments made to schema by learners as they encounter events which disturb their current understandings and lead them to new explanations and a reorganization of the relevant schema. Sarah Meadows (1993: 203) usefully describes equilibration as 'the momentary non-functioning of a cognitive scheme [schema] which both signals the presence of a "perturbation" and is the sole motivator of efforts to seek a new equilibrium'.

Development is emphasized by Piaget to explain the way that very young children deal with events in qualitatively different ways from older learners. For example, they are much more likely to resort to intuition because they cannot hold two pieces of information in their minds and connect them. The thinking of very young children can, therefore, be seen to resemble a slide presentation in which each event is discrete. Only as they mature as thinkers do children develop the capacity to look backwards and forwards, to see life as more like a video and to make connections between distinct experiences. Stories and shared experiences which help recall and anticipation are therefore important for children at this stage of their development.

Piaget's basic research question was 'How does knowledge develop in the minds of young children?'. Without a doubt he answered that question. He did not, however, ask the question 'How do children learn to participate knowledgeably in their cultures?'. If that question interests us we need to turn to sociocultural psychology for help.

Children as social thinkers

We have already answered part of the question in our discussion of learning in context. In this section we focus on some of the processes children engage in as they get to grips with the world and the interpretations that others make of it. Key words here are *intermental*, *appropriation* and *collaboration*. The sources of these ideas are found in the work of Vygotsky whose short life ended in Moscow in 1934 and have been developed since by others who share Vygotsky's interest in how we can assist children as learners.

Intermental is used by Vygotskians to mean 'between minds', and reminds us of the social basis of human knowledge and its public display in our talk and actions. Vygotsky suggested that we learn by experiencing knowledge on what he called two *planes*: the social (intermental) plane and the individual (intramental) plane. In other words we first come into contact with knowledge through experiencing how others make sense of it but we then make it our own by connecting it to our existing understandings of the world by using it and testing it. Learners' understandings and actions can be guided both by others, who are able to highlight what is useful to select from the array of stimuli available to them, and by learners' own observations of how others in their knowledge communities behave.

A disposition to engage with the knowledge available is therefore clearly an advantage. But Vygotskians also emphasize the importance of language to learning, arguing that it assists the transfer of knowledge to the individual plane and eventual internalization. You might ask whether such a process is rather like the chicken and the egg. How can learners use language without understanding what it means? The answer to that question lies in appropriation.

Appropriation is the term used to describe what learners do when they use the language of their knowledge communities without necessarily understanding it in the way that more expert members do. This is often evident in imaginative role play where children assume the language and mannerisms of the role and can be heard to *ventriloquize* the language of familiar adults. Appropriation of language occurs alongside imitation of behaviour and both appropriation and imitation help young children cope effectively with their worlds.

Observations in Alison's construction area produced several examples of younger children appropriating the language and imitating the behaviour of the older ones. For example, Harriet, aged barely 3, picked up a pencil and paper and joined Connor and Ahmed in their mark-making record of their measurements of their boat. Jonty, also 3, after observing the older boys, selected the larger blocks from the containers and made a 'pirate ship' with them.

Appropriation, together with imitation, is a very useful step in the journey towards individual understanding. Appropriation of the language used by others gives children access to the cultural tools that we outlined earlier and gives them experience of approaching tasks in the ways that their knowledge communities do.

Encouraging appropriation does, however, demand attention to role play and how it is resourced. It also requires the provision of a language-rich environment in which adults now and then think aloud order to reveal how they are interpreting and responding to what is going on, so offering children the language formats that they can in turn ventriloquize when doing something similar. The importance of offering language in this way in home settings was made clear in the study by Wells (1985) discussed earlier in this chapter, which showed a strong positive relationship between the rate of language development at 30 months and the proportion of speech directed by mothers to the child in shared activities.

Shared experiences do seem to be a key to children's early development as thinkers. In pre-school settings these experiences are often created through neighbourhood walks and visits. From these activities, opportunities for recall and reconstruction are offered by collections of photographs taken while walking or visiting which are used as focuses for shared conversations. These conversations, which move the child's thinking back to the past and forward to anticipate future events, assist young children's development as thinkers in their cultures.

Collaboration between caregiver and infant is, as we have already outlined, the source of children's initial learning. We also know from studies of older children that constructive (as opposed to, for example, argumentative) collaboration, which allows children to build understandings together, also helps children develop as thinkers (Phillips 1985; Mercer 1995, 1996). However, gauging whether pre-school children are able to collaborate fruitfully is difficult. In order to collaborate in the ways outlined by Phillips and by Mercer, children need to understand that other people might see and interpret the same thing in different ways from them, and in trying to make sense of that difference children develop their own thinking. This is quite an advanced thinking skill, requiring children to have senses of themselves as separate from others, who will in their turn be separate selves with their own interpretations, feelings and motives.

It is easy to both under- and overestimate children's abilities in this area. Judy Dunn's interesting work on children in their families from the age of 2 (Dunn 1988) has shown that from the third year of life children can be aware of the individual emotions and desires of close family members and respond appropriately. The ability to take the perspective of others develops during the pre-school period and our understanding of its development has been increased by recent work on autistic children's *theory of mind* – that is, children's capacity to recognize that others will not just have separate feelings but also separate cognitions and so see things differently from them.

One way of assessing whether children have a theory of mind is to tell them stories in which one character believes something the children know is false, such as where an object is hidden. If children predict the character's action by recognizing that the character will follow the mistaken belief they can be said to have a reasonably well-developed theory of the minds of others (see, for example, Frith 1989). Children's responses to this form of assessment suggest that they don't usually develop a robust theory of mind before the age of 4. However, a theory of mind is an essential attribute if children are to make the most of working together. Though, of course, children develop the capacity to see other children as independent thinkers through interacting with them.

In the following example we can see how a pair of 4-year-olds in a reception class who are building a house using Duplo are beginning to explore each others' understandings and work collaboratively on the activity (the extract is taken from Ogden 1997).

Emma: Has your house got rooms with doors? Has it got three doors in the living room?

Sally: It's got one door in the living room and it's got . . .

Emma: The door you go in?

Sally: And it's one door in the back kitchen, no, it's got two doors in the back kitchen, it's actually got three doors in the back kitchen.

Emma: So that means it's got three doors, that's the kitchen.

Work on theory of mind reminds us of the need for close and continuous observations of children when they are working together so that we can assess the development of children's theories of others' minds and can plan accordingly. Putting children together is not enough. We need to consider whether they are able to make the most of working with other children and how we can help them to do so.

 ## Concluding points

We have focused on learning as a process of increasingly informed participation in the world and have discussed how adults can guide young children's participation in the learning opportunities available in preschool settings. This guidance is seen in adults' sensitive interactions with children and through their careful resourcing of areas of activity. We have emphasized a play-based approach to helping children develop as confident thinkers. In the next four chapters we use the frameworks discussed here to explore how young children develop their orientation to, and their participation in, literacy and mathematics.

 ## Suggested reading

There is a vast amount of literature on children's learning from birth to 5 and a great deal of it focuses on how children learn in their social contexts.

An excellent introduction to recent work in this field is Schaffer, H.R. (1996) *Social Development* (Oxford: Blackwell). This text is aimed at undergraduate students and combines succinct accounts of major studies with a gentle explanatory style.

A review paper by Kathy Sylva (1994) usefully outlines the research on the impact of pre-school and later schooling on children's development: 'School influences on children's development', *Journal of Child Psychology and Psychiatry*, 35(1): 135–70.

Meadows, S. (1993) *The Child as Thinker* (London: Routledge) is aimed at a student readership and is a detailed and comprehensive review of approaches to understanding children's cognitive development.

Just as detailed and focused on the first two years of life is Bremner, G. (1994) *Infancy* (Oxford: Blackwell).

Judy Dunn's (1988) study of children's social development at home, *The Beginnings of Social Understanding* (Oxford: Blackwell), is an important and highly readable classic and is full of examples of children's talk which provide insight into how very young children develop a sense of themselves and of others.

See Hughes, M. and Westgate, D. (1998) 'Teachers and other adults as talk partners for pupils in nursery and reception classes', for an interesting comparison of how various professional groups and parents talk to young children and support them as thinkers. The paper is in an excellent collection of recent work on children's learning in social contexts edited by M. Woodhead, D. Faulkner and K. Littleton entitled *Cultural Worlds of Early Childhood* (London: Routledge).

Finally, as a strong antidote to current emphasis on the *what* rather than the *how* and the *who* of learning, we recommend a general book on education written from a sociocultural perspective by one of the original advisors to the Head Start Programme. It is Bruner, J. (1996) *The Culture of Education* (Cambridge, MA: Harvard University Press).

5) Language and literacy learning

One of the long-term aims of the project was to design curriculum guidelines in literacy and mathematical thinking for very young children. The processes by which we planned to achieve this aim were to identify: what activities the practitioners in their pre-school settings defined as literacy and mathematics; the nature of their understanding of how young children learn to be literate and numerate; and the relationship between early years workers' and parents' perceptions of how young children acquire competence in language, literacy and mathematical understanding. As we explained in Chapter 3, we used an action research model in our inquiry with the 20 practitioners in the project. Inevitably as we focused on what children were learning, we were drawn into discussions about how they were learning, and about how the adults were supporting their learning. The following four chapters will draw on the researchers' and practitioners' field notes and exemplary materials. Chapters 5 and 6 will focus on language and literacy and Chapters 7 and 8 on mathematical thinking.

 Language and literacy in pre-school settings

The practitioners in the project brought with them distinctive preoccupations and discourses about language and literacy from their respective exo-system levels of working traditions as childminders, carers and educators. Uniting care and education traditions at the micro-levels of their workplaces were essentially 'female' priorities and discourse about supporting families, forging caring relationships with children and their parents or carers and promoting the social/emotional development of the children. This discourse was set against references they made to the prevailing 'male' discourse of policy changes at the macro-level couched in terms of accountability for the spending of public money and promoting learning outcomes of a much more instrumental kind – for example, those in the discourse of the *Desirable Outcomes* document (DfEE/SCAA 1996a).

This framework and its successor, *The Review of the Desirable Outcomes* (QCA 1999), were designed to lead 4-year-olds into a subject-based National Curriculum framework at school entry. For practitioners in the project with backgrounds in education (either within nursery nurse or teacher training) the goals set out in the framework were relatively easy to absorb. However, it was clear from our dialogue with practitioners from care sector backgrounds that for them the document was intimidating.

Frances, the manager of an independent day nursery, described her staff's reactions when she introduced the document at a staff meeting. One responded to the mathematics outcomes with an anguished 'I didn't even get me CSE in maths. I can't teach maths'; another to the descriptors for knowledge and understanding of the world with a worried 'I were crap at geography'. Other responses were more muted! We found that some experienced practitioners from day care settings were apologetic about their perceived lack of knowledge about educational practice and their unfamiliarity with words like 'curriculum' and 'topics'. Others took a more assertive line and argued that they did not want to be 'teachers'. For example, Sally, a deputy manager of a local authority family centre, argued cogently:

> Some of our 4-year-olds are here with us for a long day. They've got all their school years ahead of them. We're not teachers. None of us has been trained how to teach a child to write their name, or read, or count. We did the basic things on NNEB courses; but we are not teachers and we don't feel qualified to teach those kind of things to the children. You hear horror stories about nurseries teaching the children the alphabet and then teachers have to re-teach them sounds – you know, they've been taught 'ay, bee, cee' and they want 'a, b, k' – and we're not teachers. But we can give them all the opportunities they need to prepare them for school.

In fact the children in this setting were offered well-planned and stimulating activities covering a broad range of learning opportunities. There was evidence of the experienced staff responding quickly to and extending children's spontaneous episodes of learning. Again, Sally, the deputy manager clearly articulated the strengths of the provision for children's learning in the centre:

We don't do much formal in the centre . . . but we cover the six [*Desirable Outcomes for Learning*] areas in play. We do science experiments. But we don't have the 4-year-olds coming out to do tracing or worksheets or whatever. It's all done through fun, practical, play activities – tie-dying, baking, whatever.

At first the staff panicked when confronted with the requirements of an education-based curriculum. Their confidence in what they were achieving was undermined. Fortunately, an experienced early years adviser in the local authority reassured them that what they were offering the children was fine.

This episode gives us an insight into the fact that curriculum models are socially constructed. They are designed by adults with particular beliefs about what constitute appropriate activities for children at a particular moment in history. The beliefs of these adults emanate from the dominant values of the culture and society at the macro-level of Bronfenbrenner's model (see Figure 1.1, page 17) within which they live and work. But most significant in shaping their beliefs about what children should do and learn before school are the culture and ideologies of their training, professional backgrounds and daily work experiences at the micro-level of their early childhood workplace settings.

It was the distinctive belief systems of 'education' that were exemplified in the 1996 *Desirable Outcomes for Learning* definition of what young children should learn:

The desirable outcomes are goals for learning for children by the time they enter compulsory education. They emphasise early literacy, numeracy and the development of personal and social skills and contribute to children's knowledge, understanding and skills in other areas. Presented as six areas of learning, they provide a foundation for later achievement.

(DfEE/SCAA 1996a: 1)

It is not surprising that those project members whose backgrounds were outside education felt threatened by the tone of *Desirable Outcomes for Learning*. The words were hard-edged – goals, compulsory education, literacy, numeracy, knowledge, understanding, skills, achievement. The definition was couched in terms of a 'high status' framework of preparation for academic achievements. Its focus was on the mind.

Contrast this set of goals for young children with one from the National Children's Bureau, where ideologies about childhood are framed in broader terms. The National Children's Bureau promotes the view that practitioners should draw families and communities into concerns about young children's development in a much more holistic way, and not just focus on their educational needs. A description of an appropriate curriculum for young children from one of their community of practitioners is 'investigation and exploration, walks and puddles and cuddles, books and blankets and anything that is part of a child's day, play and routines' (Rouse 1990). It is significant that there is a strong emotional component to this definition. The words used – cuddles, blankets, play – are about the physical and emotional needs of children, not just their intellectual needs. In this framework the body and the heart matter; the mind is just one part of the 'whole' child.

In the *Desirable Outcomes for Learning* (DfEE/SCAA 1996a) document 'play' was scarcely mentioned. The language used is an indication of the construction of childhood that dominates our policy in early years services in the UK. 'Happiness' and 'play' are derided by a male dominated society which emphasizes the logical, scientific aspects of learning and the power of rational thought (see Anning 1994 for further discussion of play and the legislated curriculum). Play is dismissed as trivial or time wasting. Yet we argued in Chapter 4 that for early years practitioners play is perceived as the natural vehicle by which young children learn. Fromberg (1990) reviewed significant research evidence of the contribution of play to children's development. Yet, he points out, 'at the same time that the research literature on the value of play appears to expand geometrically the presence of play in early childhood classrooms has been dwindling' (p. 237).

It is significant that education has been assigned the lead role in the government's policy on integration of services for children. Current government policies on early childhood education prioritize children's academic achievements, not their emotional and social development, nor their physical well-being. Practitioners with educational backgrounds feel secure. So during the project, we never heard those with backgrounds in educational services apologize about their lack of knowledge and understanding of children's physical and emotional needs. We think these should be priorities. Even at a pragmatic level of measuring 'success', if children are not happy and comfortable, they are unlikely to feel good about learning and to make good progress in academic achievements. Equally, from a moral and ethical point of view, young children's emotional and physical well-being should be of paramount importance. It may be that those with educational backgrounds could learn from their colleagues in the care sector about catering for aspects of children's needs which are emotional and physical.

However, it is the discourse of 'school' subjects, not of children's general well-being, which has dominated curriculum reform for young children since the Education Reform Act of 1987. Of all the 'subjects' of the school curriculum, English is the one with which early childhood workers in all kinds of pre-school settings are most comfortable. However, depending on their backgrounds and belief systems, they will approach the 'subject' in rather different ways. For example, local authority funded day care settings have a tradition of prioritizing language development in the activities they plan for their children. This emphasis is the result of the 'compensatory' framework of the care sector because, as we discussed in Chapter 1, historically their population has been skewed to 'disadvantaged' families and children 'at risk'. However, day care workers' approach to language development is very different from that in, for example, nursery classes in the maintained sector, where a particular 'school' view of language and literacy prevails. Their focus is on the development of spoken language.

The foundations of the school concept of literacy are the nineteenth-century elementary school traditions of 'reading and writing'. Children were required to learn to write in 'a fair hand', often by laboriously copying poems from the established canons of English literature or morally uplifting tracts. They had to learn the discipline of parsing sentences in order to access the syntax of the English language. They had exercises in the comprehension and paraphrasing of high-status texts. Finally they learned to read from 'primers' of the Janet and John, Dick and Dora or Peter and Jane variety! All these activities were geared to the needs of training a docile working population ready to operate in working contexts where a particular, narrow version of literacy prevailed. Much of the nostalgic call for a 'back to basics' curriculum during the 18 years of Tory government in England and Wales up until 1996 was a hankering for a return to this simplistic notion of training a docile workforce. It could be argued that New Labour policy has simply added the word 'adaptable' to the requirement!

However, even if we were to accept the questionable view that the *raison d'être* of a curriculum is to prepare children for work, such a backward looking model takes no account of the rapidly changing nature of literacy as we move into the twenty-first century. The computer, word processor, Internet and microfiche have entirely altered the notion of what it means to be literate. A broad definition of what it means to be literate as we approach the millennium was given by the National Association of the Teachers of English (NATE 1998: 1):

Individuals must be literate, in the widest possible sense, to play a full part in society in the twenty-first century, whether locally or globally. Being literate involves the ability to make meaning from texts as well as decode them. It also involves the ability to create texts. It is linked closely with oracy. The texts and technologies of the literate may be many and varied. They involve spoken and written language, electronic and print media, still and moving images. Literacy is learnt and developed through play and talk as well as reading, writing and instruction. The teaching of literacy takes account of the linear and recursive nature of learning, makes explicit what is known implicitly and is based on knowledge of pupils' emergent expertise. Teaching and learning build on and extend existing literacy practices.

Yet our education system is still geared to promoting literacy with a strong emphasis on 'conventional' reading and writing and this model is increasingly 'colonizing' pre-school settings. The sign systems of school literacy – alphabet charts, words blu-tacked onto doors, chairs and tables, workbooks and worksheets – which set the boundaries of literacy in the formal settings of many early years classrooms are infiltrating the informal settings of day care centres, childminders and even some young children's bedrooms or playrooms at home. Parents are pressurized into joining this version of 'the literacy club' by a burgeoning industry in 'out-of-school'/homework educational materials. In supermarkets parents are urged to invest in an array of workbooks, videos and educational games, all designed to improve children's basic skills in reading and writing. In 1998 all children in primary schools of compulsory school age were required to be taught a 'literacy hour' every day. From September 1998 even as children entered compulsory schooling (mostly at the age of 4) they were tested by baseline assessment systems on recognition of initial sounds in words, letters by both shape and sounds, and ability to write their names and words independently. Young children learn to position themselves within this dominant model of literacy. For example, reading is perceived to be about decoding text in books. So Scollon and Scollon (1981) report a young child explaining 'when my baby brother's hands are big enough to hold a book, he'll be able to read'.

We have to question both the appropriateness and effectiveness of this kind of curriculum model for language and literacy learning for young children. There are two aspects of the model that are questionable: the relationship of the model to what we know about children's *cognitive development* and its relationship to what we know about the most *appropriate pedagogy* for young children.

Turning to *cognitive development* first, we know that children learn to use representational systems modelled by more expert learners – either adults or older children – in the social contexts in which they learn to be literate and numerate. Children experiment with different ways of representing their growing understanding of the world around them. Bruner (1963) identified three categories of representation: enactive representations (when children participate through their actions), iconic representations (when they participate through looking at or making pictures or images of things) and symbolic representations (when they participate through using the more powerful symbols of, for example, print or mathematical symbols to represent things). Symbolic representations offer the child opportunities to move from consideration of the concrete here and now of immediate experiences to the abstraction of events that were in the past or may be in the future. The role of adults or more experienced siblings is to mediate for the child these different modes of representation until they are able to use them with confidence independently. Bruner called this mediation 'scaffolding' (see page 69 in Chapter 4).

Piagetian stage theory seemed to indicate that young children have limited capacities to think at 'abstract' levels. However, Donaldson's (1978) seminal work, *Children's Minds*, argued that children could think at a high level of complexity and in abstract terms if the problems they tackled were embedded in contexts which made sense to them on an everyday, concrete level. They were disadvantaged when confronted with problems which were 'disembedded' from their real world connections. One could argue that the kinds of 'school' literacy tasks presented to young children in print or mathematical notation form in early stages of their literacy learning were just such 'disembedded' problems. There is an argument that, by placing so much emphasis so early in a child's development on introducing them to the abstract symbolic systems of representing meaning in print and numbers, we are wrong-footing them at their most vulnerable stage of learning to be learners. At this stage they need opportunities to explore enactive and iconic representations.

The fact is that despite the current policy of promoting an early introduction to 'school' versions of literacy, British children, particularly boys, are scoring less well on measures of achievements in language and mathematics than children from systems in other European countries (for example, Hungary, Switzerland and Belgium) where pre-school experiences place an emphasis on talk and structured, active play which enable children to move more freely between enactive, iconic and symbolic modes of representation. In these countries children do not start their formal schooling with its emphasis on symbolic representation until they are 6.

Researchers for a Channel 4 programme, *Britain's Early Years Disaster*, argued that:

> The evidence suggests that Britain's early years education, far from helping young children, actually damages many of them. Unlike successful pre-school systems abroad – which move slowly from the concrete to the representational and avoid the abstract – British early years provision rushes children into abstract letters, words and numbers. While elsewhere primacy is given to developing confidence and precision in spoken language, here teaching is dominated by reading, writing and recorded arithmetic.
>
> While brighter children and those from privileged backgrounds can cope with the demands this makes, less fortunate children suffer,

lose confidence and probably never recover. It seems likely that this helps explain Britain's long tail of under-achievement.

(Mills and Mills 1998: 17)

It is not only the curriculum content that appears to be inappropriate for our young children, but also the danger that the pedagogy of early childhood will become one of curriculum delivery. The current government emphasis on 'direct instruction' and 'whole class teaching' in primary education, exemplified in the arguments for the National Literacy and Numeracy Strategies, is impacting on Reception and even some nursery classes in England and Wales. Yet we have research evidence that young children who are exposed to too formal a schooling regime too soon may suffer long-term disadvantages. Much of this evidence was summarized by three women researchers in the early 1990s when pressure was building up from central government policy to introduce more formal styles of pedagogy into primary schools (see David *et al.* 1993). For example, results of the research in the USA (Schweinhart and Weikart 1993) cited in Chapter 2, page 31, also reported by Sylva and Wiltshire (1993), indicated that three groups of children, one of which had experienced a formal pre-school curriculum and the other two play-based programmes (one a curriculum called High Scope and another less structured programme similarly based on active learning) showed increased IQs at school entry. However, in a follow-up study of the three groups at the age of 15, those that had attended the formal programme engaged more in antisocial behaviour and had lower commitment to school than those from the play-based programmes. In a more recent paper Sylva (1997) again used research-based evidence to argue that 'a curriculum in pre-school settings that is too formal will lead to poorer performance, disincentives to learn and low self-esteem' (p. 4). This takes us back to the issues raised in Chapter 4 about the significance of promoting positive 'dispositions' in the crucial formative stages of children learning to be learners, including learning to be readers, writers and speakers.

Alternative approaches to literacy

So if 'school' models of language and literacy are inappropriate for under-5s, what models might be appropriate?

Chomsky (1976) argued that human beings are born with an innate ability to acquire language. He called this inborn mechanism a 'language acquisition device'. He argued that children build on their innate ability to learn language through interaction with the people around them and through engaging with everyday events and objects. Chomsky's work was crucial in developing our understanding of how individual children develop competence in language. However, in this project we have taken a *social-interactionist approach* to learning language and literacy. This approach is based on the view that the context scaffolds children's developing competence and that children are intentional communicators from very early on. The social and cultural setting in which a child acquires competence in talking, listening, reading and writing is as important as his or her individual developing competence in spoken language, or the ability to decode print, or to represent thinking in written form. Our approach acknowledges the active and purposeful role of babies in engaging adults in communication and the importance of the adult carer providing a language acquisition support system (Whitehead 1990). Essentially, young children are motivated to use language formats in order to gain attention or to achieve some goal. Whitehead described the process: 'Children learn to be social beings and language users in close partnership and collaborations with caring adults and other children who participate eagerly with them in the adventure of reconstructing a language for getting things done' (1990: 50).

In Chapter 4 we saw how Ivy's work with babies, involving both parents and carers in a day care setting, provided this kind of support to promote communication between babies and the adults who cared for them. Our approach acknowledged the importance of the pre-verbal communication system – gestures and sounds – established between babies and adults and siblings as a prerequisite for the development of language. These gestures and sounds, or early language formats, form a bridge to communication based on speech. They often take the form of games – for example, peek-a-boo or making growling or squeaking noises with soft toys.

However, *music* can be an important pre-verbal mode of communication too. Three members of the project (Frances, Millie and Jade) instinctively based much of their investigation on the role of songs and rhymes in very young children's learning. Frances used singing in many of her interactions with children. She described herself as 'a bit of a Pied Piper'. She was aware that singing and simple poems gave young children opportunities to communicate with adults and in small groups through sounds and speech, but without the pressure of meaning making. The sounds in the songs and rhymes provided the children with 'scripts' to practise listening, making eye contact, turn-taking and responding.

Unless children are secure in the environment of a *rich oral culture* – what Egan (1988: 86) describes as 'the lore and language, play and games, fantasy and story of young children' – their journey into literacy will be impoverished. Egan argues that 'sounds' of orality are powerful modes of binding generations together into shared understandings. He also urges adults to surround children with 'authentic' learning experiences rather than patronize them with what he describes as a 'baby safe' curriculum of activities designed exclusively for children. Interestingly,

when Jade used songs as a mode for encouraging home/school collaboration with Somali and Yemeni families, she discovered that the
concept of 'nursery rhymes' was not familiar to them. In their domestic
lives everyone sang the same songs and heard the same music – lullabies
for sleeping, religious chants for worship, rhythmical music for dancing. They did not have 'special' songs for children. Egan (1988: 86–7)
wrote:

> We use endless formulae to impress an array of behaviour patterns
> on children, for road safety, cutlery and utensil use, care of toys and
> furniture etc. We recite proverbs, tell stories, teach rhymes, tell
> jokes etc. These all help to build the mental structures that systemat-
> ise memory and poeticise the prosaic world, creating imaginative
> space and power to be enchanted by magic and ecstasy. If we begin
> to think of the objectives of our early childhood curriculum as tied
> up with magic and ecstasy, with imagination . . . we might see our
> way to making literacy, numeracy, and rationality richer and more
> meaningful attainments.

The telling of *stories* is another important feature of a language acquisition support system. Familiarity with the structures of narrative forms –
beginnings, middles and ends of stories – helps children to learn how to
sequence ideas, remember the constituent parts of a series of past events
and predict or anticipate what might happen to them in the future. In
other words, stories provide for children a way of helping them think
beyond the here and now of their immediate experiences to make that
important leap to connections with a more distanced, abstract past or
future (see Wells 1987; Wade 1993).

Oral storying is often a rich and engaging feature of a family's everyday
life – the banter about family rituals and quirks of character, the gossip
on the telephone, the 'pub' talk, the recapping on the current soap
opera crises. Children growing up in environments characterized by rich-
ness of oral language are drawn into a community of 'storying' and then
replicate storying behaviours in their play. Paley (1986: 124) reported
her eavesdropping on such a community of young fluent speakers:

> The children sounded like groups of actors, rehearsing spontaneous
> skits on a moving stage, blending into one another's plots, carrying
> on philosophical debates while borrowing freely from the fragments
> of dialogue that floated by. Themes from fairy tales and television
> cartoons mixed easily with social commentary and private fantas-
> ies, so that what to me often sounded random and erratic formed a
> familiar and comfortable world for the children.

Storying based on books is another key experience for young children
learning to be literate. If adults read stories to children, at bedtime at

home or in story reading sessions in playgroups, they are inducting children into the fun of book behaviours as well as the conventions of print. Fiction has a particular set of linguistic conventions: for example, 'Once upon a time' and 'So they all lived happy ever after'. Gaining familiarity with these conventions helps children to 'tune into' the kind of reading and writing they will be expected to do when they start school.

Heath's (1982, 1983) study of the language use of families in different communities in the USA identified that families defined as middle class were more likely to model the kind of 'learning and displays of knowledge expected in school' (Heath 1982: 51). In many of the families in her study defined as working class, encounters with books or what she described as 'major literacy events' for the children were more likely to be based on didactic-style reading of alphabet or number books or Bible stories. Inevitably those children who are familiar with the rituals of 'school' story reading are at an advantage when starting school.

So we can see that what counts as literacy is co-constructed in the minds of parents or carers, teachers and children and that versions of literacy are dependent on the social contexts in which they are enacted. For example, the rituals of book-based reading will be very different when a parent is reading a child a bedtime story, or when a playgroup worker is reading a story to a group of children sitting on a mat before 'home time', or when a teacher is listening to a child reading from her or his reading scheme book.

The project team took the view that the model of beginning *reading* that most benefits young children is not the 'disembedded' learning of letter sounds and names and the completion of phonic-based worksheets, but reading within the context of enjoying story and picture books, and delighting in the telling and retelling of familiar fairy stories and rhymes. Playing with sounds, rhythms and words whets children's appetite for learning about all aspects of language.

We also took the view that children learn much of their literacy before school from opportunities to engage with functional literacy in everyday situations – recognizing well-known signs and symbols as well as significant words and numbers from everyday life: Coke bottle signs, supermarket logos, car registration numbers, street signs, letters and numbers on the TV screen. A letter K becomes associated with a favourite cereal and the Little Chef logo with a break in car journeys for a meal. Children are exposed to all kinds of information systems – sounds, signs, lists, moving images on computer or television screens. They are exposed from babyhood to a world of multi-modality and multi-literacy. In comparison, the world of 'letteracy' in school must seem rather dull.

As for *writing*, again we took a much broader view of communication through graphic form than that associated with 'school' writing. Young children's attempts to externalize their understanding may take the form of mark-making, manipulating objects, making models, drawing or role play behaviours. We were informed particularly by the work of Kress (1997) who argues that 'Children act multi-modally, both in the things they use, the objects they make; and in their engagement of their bodies; there is no separation of body and mind' (p. 97). It is through these multi-modal representations of their understanding that young children move confidently towards literacy.

Young children move freely between expressing themselves through spoken language, mark-making, making models, manipulating objects in role play and physical movements. Athey's (1990) work on schemas developed the idea of 'patterns of repeatable behaviour into which experiences are assimilated and that are gradually co-ordinated' (p. 37). She categorized the types of schemas she observed 2- to 5-year-old children using in nursery and home settings – for example, 'dynamic circular', 'enclosure', 'developing and containing space', 'dynamic vertical'. She claimed that schemas exemplified in children's mark-making were replicated in their play behaviours. So, for example, if a child were preoccupied with a 'dynamic circular' schema, she or he could be observed repeatedly drawing circles, playing in sand and water using circular movements, rolling a ball, rotating and staring at wheels on bikes or prams or running in circles, and would be particularly interested in songs (such as 'Round and Round the Garden') or stories (such as 'The Enormous Turnip') in which circular shapes figured.

Children's first experiments with *mark-making* are for kinaesthetic pleasure – making patterns on their high-chair tray with jam-covered fingers or later moving crayons across the surface of paper (Matthews 1994). As when adults shape babies' babbling into speech sounds by feeding back to them with delight sounds that approximate to words (mum, mum mum or da da da) so adults feed back interest in the marks children make when they begin to create more controlled patterns. So a circular scribble becomes a face and horizontal and vertical marks become a house. The child is encouraged to make the crucial shift to using marks to represent things by the reactions of adults or other children around them.

However, while they are being socialized into the use of conventional forms of representation, children continue to explore their own personal and essentially private agenda through making compositions which often involve accompanying talk and actions (Anning 1999). Some of their marks represent sounds (the pitter patter of rain may be dashes), or movement (the path of a spaceship represented by a long sweeping line), or emotions (dark, frenzied scribbling to black out the figure of a newly-born rival sibling). These marks are the visual equivalent of dramatic play where objects (cushions, tablecloths, pieces of furniture, soft toys) become the physical manifestations of the child's imaginative world.

There have been some detailed studies of the unique pathways young children have taken towards drawing capability, usually documented by parents (for example, Matthews 1994).

There are parallel detailed longitudinal studies of children's journeys towards literacy (for example, Bissex 1980; Baghban 1984; Laminack 1991). Children learn about *writing* by watching adults and older children writing. Their mark-making approximations that lead to letter shapes therefore reflect the configurations of the writing that are dominant in the culture in which they are growing up. Gregory's (1996, 1998) research on young bilingual children cites some examples of young children's emergent writing in two versions of scripts at both home and school. Children's approximations of letters are gradually shaped into recognizable letters, which are then combined into words and then sentences. Their first written words are those that are related to their burgeoning sense of self and to key relationships or objects in their everyday lives – their own names, significant TV characters, favourite animals, key members of the family (see Hall 1987).

Children then have to learn sound/letter relationships in order for them to be able to invent novel letter sequences which convey meaning to other people. Two key research programmes investigating how children develop understanding of the alphabetic nature of writing systems were reported by Clay (1975) and Ferreiro and Teberovsky (1982). They charted young children's attempts to create messages. Children use letter names to convey speech sounds – for example the famous note pushed in front of Bissex (1980) by her young son when she repeatedly ignored his attempts to get her attention: 'RUDF' (Are you deaf?). Children use mainly consonants at first. Vowels appear later. They tend to group letters into units of three or four to make their first 'words'. As their knowledge of written language grows, they gain increasing confidence in making their messages clear. Adults play a crucial role in being the audience for such messages and in responding to them with written or spoken replies. It is important for adults to encourage children in their initial idiosyncratic attempts at 'emergent writing' and to guide them gently towards the conventions of print.

It is also important to encourage children to experiment freely with communicating through drawing, making models and making images on computer screens. By the time our young children are adults, literacy will look very different. Increasing reliance on information retrieval systems which use diagrams, sounds and both still and moving images to convey meaning will generate very different demands on the next generation of writers. As Kress (1997: 142) argues 'The world into which children will move will be a world of multi-modality and multi-literacy. It will demand such skills and dispositions as part of an adaptable, innovative workforce'.

The co-construction of a new literacy curriculum

The problem for practitioners in informal, non-school settings, as many in our project were, is that as yet there is no identifiable 'discourse' about learning in their professional literature. As Munn (1994a) pointed out, before children enter schooling the curriculum will often be based on activities that are about practical skills (such as learning to get shoes on and off), social skills (such as taking turns in card or board games) or about learning the routines of being in an institutional setting (such as eating together). Such 'knowledge' has not been codified and is often dismissed as 'trivial'. In order to give such knowledge status, educators work backwards from 'school' knowledge and retrospectively justify these activities in educational terms. Munn gives the following examples:

- buttoning up coats involves one-to-one correspondence and therefore maps onto counting;
- tying shoelaces involves spatial awareness and therefore maps onto mathematical development;
- distinguishing colours and shapes involves perceptual discrimination and therefore maps onto reading.

As she points out, 'By such extrapolation, cognitive aspects of the pre-school curriculum are created from basic tasks and an educational discourse is constructed' (Munn 1994a: 7).

However, this construction of an 'educational discourse' leaves early years workers from non-school settings feeling disempowered. It may also mean that they do not engage with formal curriculum documents. In Blenkin and Kelly's (1997) analysis of returns from a range of settings providing for children from birth to 8 within their *Principles into Practice in Early Childhood Education* project, many practitioners, including those from Key Stage 1 settings, did not respond to the question 'How would you describe a quality curriculum for young children?' Others simply appended local authority or national guidelines for curriculum coverage. The documents had become a reason not to think any more.

What was important for us was to try to promote an exchange of ideas between practitioners from non-school and nursery education settings about a new version of the curriculum which would not dismiss routine activities as 'trivial' or recast them as 'preparation for school learning'. We wanted to build on the knowledge and expertise embedded in their work-place practices, rather than base a dialogue on imported, disembedded curriculum models. We wanted to co-construct a curriculum from their authentic work-based practices.

In order to confront the similarities and differences between the perceptions of the care- and education-based practitioners in the project, and to confront the prejudices each may have had about each other's work-based practices, it was important that each sector had direct access to evidence of what the other actually did in promoting literacy. Only when assumptions were confronted by evidence could defensive posturing and mutual suspicion begin to break down. It is to this evidence, and to the role of the adults – both at home and in pre-school settings – in promoting children's learning in language and literacy that we turn in Chapter 6.

 ## Suggested reading

A comprehensive introduction to language and literacy education in the early years is Marian Whitehead's *Language and Literacy in the Early Years: An Approach for Education Students* (Paul Chapman Publishing Ltd: 1990).

Eve Gregory's edited collection *One Child, Many Worlds: Early Learning in Multi-cultural Communities*, published by David Fulton in 1997 includes 11 case studies of children aged 3 to 8 in a range of cultures (UK and international) entering the culture and language of schooling.

For the beginnings of reading and writing, Robin Campbell's short but accessible *Literacy in Nursery Education* published by Trentham Books in 1996, sets out models of good practice in nursery schools. Linda Miller's more comprehensive *Towards Reading*, published by Open University Press in 1996 brings together recent research on early literacy development and implications for practitioners. For the beginnings of writing both Nigel Hall's (1987) seminal book on *The Emergence of Literacy* published by Hodder & Stoughton and the more recent book by Gunther Kress, *Before Writing: Rethinking the Paths to Literacy*, published by Routledge in 1997 are both excellent.

Gordon Wells' (1981) edited collection *Learning through Interaction: The Study of Language Development*, published by Cambridge University Press, is a good introduction to language development in young children.

6 How adults support children's literacy learning

In each of the diverse settings where the project team worked on Step 2 (see Figure 3.1, page 37) of the action research cycle they began by collecting evidence of literacy activities in the workplace and considering how these compared to the children's language experiences in the informal learning contexts of home. Their first surprise was how much was currently going on in their normal working activities with very young children that corresponded to the broad definition of literacy set out in Chapter 5. So we found that there was much to build on in the *what* content of 'everyday' literacy activities in their daily interactions with babies, toddlers and 'pre-school' children: enjoying books together, mark-making in role play areas, chatting about the daily routines around snacks, washing their hands, tidying up the toys and equipment, setting off for walks to the shops.

There was less confidence about how to structure and organize the *how* of the curriculum – how to plan for enrichment activities without losing the spontaneity and enthusiasm shown by the children for self-chosen tasks; how to monitor and record children's progress in a way that was both useful and manageable; how to improve the quality of staff/children interactions; how to share understandings of emergent literacy with parents/carers.

However, the important thing was that all the questions raised were based on the documentary evidence of observations of staff and children working together in authentic contexts and under the real constraints of the hectic nature of working in pre-school settings. These questions were the starting points for the second cycle of action research when 'hunches' about possible answers were tested against further evidence gathered during Step 3 of the project.

Two such starting points are illustrated in the descriptions of projects given below. They were set in very different types of settings, and illustrate, in summary:

- how two practitioners worked through the action research cycle towards clarifying their approach to developing a literacy curriculum for very young children;
- the important principle of involving work colleagues in the processes of action research and working closely with them to manage change;
- the principle of involving parents in young children's development and learning.

 ## Example 1

Frances was the manager of a thriving workplace nursery. She had initiated a shift from family grouping into areas for separate age groups: for example, areas for under-2s and over-2s. In 1998 we found such regrouping of children into same-age 'bands' common in early years/family centres, as staff prepared for Ofsted inspections focused on their 'delivery' of the 1996 *Desirable Outcomes for Learning* (DfEE/SCAA 1996a). The regrouping of the children had created a great upheaval in the nursery, and Frances was aware that the staff were keen to monitor the effects of the reorganization on the children. For example, one of the anxieties about the 'banding' of children was that it might restrict their flexibility in reorganizing age groups during daily routines.

Frances set up a meeting between herself and two members of staff. They discussed their concerns about some children's lack of turn-taking and listening skills and the possibility of using an expanded repertoire of singing, action rhymes and percussion work to improve them. Notes in her research diary show a clear sense of purpose: 'Our aim was to value and expand our children's ability to listen, communicate and interact'.

The vehicle they chose to achieve this aim was music. Frances believed passionately that music was undervalued in young children's learning. She believed that singing and making music had great potential to provide 'scripts' for communicating in speech, encouraging children to listen carefully and extending their ability to pay attention for longer periods. In fact there is research evidence that learning nursery rhymes, clapping rhythms and playing action and marching games encourages children to listen for and recognize rhymes and rhythms in speech. These skills help them later to acquire the more formal knowledge of phonics and syllables in words in the beginning stages of learning to read (see Bryant and Bradley 1985; Goswami and Bryant 1990).

One of the 'hunches' the two members of staff wanted to test was whether older children offering models of more 'expert' listening, turn-taking and singing or making music in mixed-age activities was beneficial to the younger children. They began to observe the under- and over-2s, sometimes singing together as a mixed group, sometimes in much smaller same-age groups. Examples of their dated observations are given below. They were collated by Frances as the starting point for discussion at the next staff meeting.

> Mixed ages and target children held hands and sang 'Ring-O-Roses'. Sat in a circle to sing five more songs together. All happy except G (aged 1) who crawled away after one song. Distracting to have younger children when I'm working with my target group (Laura: 19.8.97).

> Children all gathered on the carpet. Sang 'Twinkle Twinkle', 'Heads and Shoulders', 'If You're Happy and You Know It'. All eager to join in. I did the actions wrong once or twice to see if they'd notice – the older children did! I watched who knew the actions and who didn't. Lots of fun. Then we went on to some number games: 'Five Little Astronauts', 'Five Currant Buns'. Enjoyed the first one, but then they started to get distracted. They could see the new toys being put out for the after dinner activities. I observed it was much easier to hold their attention when everyone was joining me with the actions rather than some watching others do things (Ruth: 12.8.98).

In her notes, Frances, as the manager of the nursery, indicated the complex relationship between improving the quality of children's learning experiences and planning for the professional development of individual members of a staff team. In her notebook she wrote:

> I wanted to ensure collaboration between the rooms and see that a chasm did not occur. I also felt sure the link for the rising 2s would be excellent. The two key staff I had selected had not had the opportunity to work closely together and since they were both strong characters, I hoped they would influence others.

The staff shared their notes at a second meeting. They began to see patterns in children's behaviours in both the mixed- and single-aged groupings. Frances wrote:

> We noticed differences in which children were able or willing to join in the activities and remember the words/sounds. We noted who had the confidence to sing alone in the small same-age groups but not in the larger group. We were surprised at how quickly they all grasped the rituals of sitting in a circle or the actions of the finger rhymes in the mixed-age groupings. We began to note changes in behaviour of children at story times who were now beginning to listen better. Did Lauren do so well in settling to stories now because she'd been part of our target singing group? Or was she just ready to be attentive in a group story time now?

The singing activities led to a book of nursery songs and rhymes being printed for the parents so that they could enjoy at home the songs and rhymes the children were learning in the nursery. The book became a point of contact when these busy working parents came to collect their children. On a superficial level the talk around handing the songbooks backwards and forwards between parents and practitioners was about non-threatening, fun activities that they could all share in and enjoy; but the chatting gave opportunities to raise some significant issues about individual children's learning and development for staff and parents. For example, Frances noted an exchange between herself and the parent of a particularly confident singer – so confident that despite her small stature she had been observed frequently directing other children at music making or singing times. The child's father was able to play an instrument. The child was due to leave the nursery shortly because a second baby was due in the family. It was during these informal exchanges about the song book that he promised to encourage her love of music in every way possible.

The focus on music led to the two members of staff setting up a rhythm station in a corridor for children and parents to explore sound together. Staff also set up a tape deck so that children could select and play their favourite music. The staff negotiated with some local businesses to sponsor the production of some large 'song and game mats' to lay out in corridor areas used for large motor play when it was too wet or cold to play outside. At all stages of the project observations were made of the children using these new resources to feed back into the next phase of planning. Photographs and video recordings were used to supplement field note observations. The cycle of planning, recording, evaluating and replanning meant that the curriculum experiences offered to the children were constantly being improved or refined. A section of a display board for parents in the nursery entrance hall kept them informed of what the staff were finding out about the children and their music making. The parents and staff planned an evening of seventies music together. In her final evaluation of the project Frances noted:

> Our aim to value and expand our children's ability to listen, communicate and interact has been achieved. But music now has a higher profile in the nursery with a variety of practical games/props to use. We also have a staff team who are I believe more aware of the huge benefits music can make to everyone's lives.

 Example 2

Meg was the manager of a very different setting, an inner-city early years centre. She had a clear vision of the role of the centre:

The children's development and education are not looked at in isolation. The child is part of a family unit and the community in which s/he lives. We consider our role as one of family supporters and educators of children.

Through questionnaires and informal discussions with parents about their approaches to supporting their children's development, Meg understood that they did not want to be involved in working with their children in the centre. She discovered that they made little use of the local library. However, it was clear that they wanted the best start in life for their children.

The records and monitoring systems in the centre showed that a high percentage of the children had poor social skills and behaviour problems. They also had poor speech, listening and comprehension skills. They showed little evidence of having handled books or of positive attitudes towards them.

Meg decided to take up a local authority initiative to support early years centres in setting up book loan schemes for families. She saw it as a way of addressing several challenges: stimulating the children to enjoy books, involving parents in their children's early literacy learning, and providing a vehicle to enhance the communication between staff and parents/carers.

The book loan scheme proved to be a great success with the parents. It gave plenty of opportunities for the staff to capitalize on the good informal relationships they had built up with parents. As with the chat around the songbooks in Frances' setting, the chat around the weekly early morning session set aside for selecting and returning books provided non-stigmatized opportunities for dialogue between staff and parents about many aspects of children's development, but particularly about sharing books with them. In this context (as in Frances', where parents were in full-time work) setting up 'workshops' to support parents in 'how to teach children about reading' would have 'frightened parents off'. Instead they designed some simple, non-jargon prompt sheets for parents to take home when they were choosing books. Such informal, user-friendly support for the parents worked well. The prompt sheets included such suggestions as:

- find quiet moments for sharing books;
- even babies enjoy playing with books – they won't tear them if you show them how to hold them;
- don't nag if you're both not enjoying it – stop and try again another time.

Meg noted at the end of several months of monitoring the book loan scheme:

Children are instigating conversations about books they've read at home with parents. They are eager to borrow new books and ask 'Is it book loan today?' Parents are saying things like 'I must have read this three hundred times! I know it off by heart'. There is a notice-able improvement in how children are handling books in the centre. The book loan sessions have offered opportunities for parents to talk about their own literacy and how they can extend the help they have been giving when their children learn to read and write. It has offered them opportunities to discuss concerns they have about their children's language and speech. Books have also helped them over difficult issues to deal with – bed wetting, potty training, sharing, daddy leaving home etc.

Once the book loan scheme was firmly established, the staff wanted to introduce something new to the scheme. When one of the researchers mentioned the power of nursery rhymes in young children's develop-ment towards literacy, the staff decided to introduce nursery rhyme cards into the loan scheme. The rhymes were word processed in large type onto colourful cards and suggestions for shared activities between the parent/carer and child were added to the back of each card. Sugges-tions included actions to accompany the rhymes, finding familiar words together, pointing along the lines as you sing the words, missing out some words and letting the child add them, making up some 'silly' alternative rhymes of your own. (The latter suggestion was given the thumbs down by the parents as too hard!)

Particularly full records were kept of a 3-year-old child, Mandy, a child referred by social services, and her parents' responses to the books and nursery rhyme cards loan scheme. Mandy's parents said that they had not enjoyed reading at school and were not confident readers now. For them reading aloud to Mandy did not bring back happy memories at first, but as they pointed out, 'at home no one can hear you'. Mandy was very demanding of her parents' attention and often had temper tantrums. Sharing books provided a point of contact between her and her parents. As Meg noted:

> When there are difficulties at home that are not child-centred, it is hard at times for Mandy to compete for attention. The books help her parents to focus attention on Mandy. Mandy has also realized that one way of gaining her parents attention as an alternative to temper tantrums is using books. Her parents have also used sharing books as a way of calming her down. They have found 'Bartholomew's Potty' a real help; the knowledge that potty training and temper tantrums are not unique to Mandy. 'Bartholomew's Potty' is about saying no, no, no. The big teddy in the story stays calm throughout (parent role model?) and lets Bartholomew get on with it. Eventually

he uses the potty . . . The close contact that reading together requires, sitting on your knee, making eye contact, cuddling up together, has helped the relationship between Mandy and her parents. The book loan and the rhyme cards have allowed the child and parents to play together. When an adult is presented with a toy to play with a child, the role of the adult is not easily defined. A toy is a child's domain and the adult may not feel comfortable with it. Sharing a book is much more a natural shared activity.

Comments from Mandy's parents included:

She will try to make up the story she sees in the pictures in her own words. I read the book first then Mandy tries to read it to me. She will try sounds and copy me. She has never done this before. She was having to see a speech therapist.

The nursery rhyme cards are good. She now sings all the time. We didn't know many nursery rhymes before but we do now.

At the end of the project Meg reviewed the impact of the book and rhyme cards loan scheme on the centre. Key findings were:

The setting up of the book loan and the introduction of the rhyme cards did not produce instant results. Far more important was the consistency of the twice a week sessions and the availability of a member of staff to promote discussion with the parents and value and respect their views. However, there was an increase in parents' interest in their children's ability to become literate and they were increasingly observant about what their children could do; for example, 'She can recognize the first letter of her name now'. It allowed children to make choices about books and stimulated their curiosity about them. Some children have started to bring their own books into the centre with them. The dialogue with parents gave the staff the opportunity to value early years education in its own right, not just as a stopgap while children are waiting to go to school.

There is plenty of research evidence that involving parents in young children's literacy learning through home visits and workshops is bene-ficial for children's confidence and competence as beginning readers and writers. See, for example, Weinberger's work in Sheffield (Weinberger *et al.* 1990); work done in Birmingham within the Shopping to Read Programme (Strongin Dodds 1994); the Basic Skills Agency's family lit-eracy programmes evaluated by the National Foundation for Educa-tional Research in 1994–5 (Brooks *et al.* 1996). However, the work of Meg and her staff is a fine example of how staff in an early childhood setting which has by tradition been more focused on care than educa-tion can acknowledge and build on what parents do at home. As Strongin

Dodds (1994: 12) argued, parents can, by informal but highly skilled intervention, be empowered to be significant 'teachers' of their children if they are given appropriate support: 'It is not that they lack the initiative, but they are uncertain about the practicalities of teaching their children'.

As we pointed out at the beginning of this chapter it was the 'practicalities of teaching', the *how* adults support children's learning to be literate, that most taxed the early years workers in the project. We shall examine how they set about exploring their roles as educators using as an organizing framework the age phases members of the team chose to focus on (see Table 3.1, page 38): birth to 18 months, 18 months to 3 years and 3 years to 5 years.

 ## Birth to 18 months

Communication through speaking and listening

Ivy managed an early years centre set in a deprived inner-city area. She had a social worker background. In her project an important premise was that parents were offered support in a way that was respectful of, rather than a denial of, their personal and domestic realities. Many of the families in the community were beset by multiple difficulties with housing, money and relationships. Ivy was concerned about the effects of acute depression, suffered by some of her most vulnerable parents, on their communication with their babies. In her notes she wrote:

> I want to develop in parents the skills and knowledge that they are the ones best able to facilitate their own children's development. It is also important to acknowledge and understand the stress and pressures on individual families.

Ivy was also concerned that her staff were not generally given effective training in how to work with babies. Her experience was that qualifications and courses tend to emphasize training early years workers for the needs of 3-year-olds and upwards. Thus, though Ivy made her project focus communication skills between mothers and babies, the centre's development plan included upgrading staff expertise in their communication with babies.

Ivy targeted six mothers categorized as having learning difficulties themselves or whose babies were identified as 'at risk'. Although she was extremely competent and confident in how to work with families from her social work perspective, she felt less sure about her understanding of how to promote language development with babies. Wisely, she drew on the expertise of colleagues in the meso-system of the community of practice around the centre: the speech therapist attached to the centre, the health visitor, the course tutor from the speech therapy department of the local college and a local nursery teacher. Between them they designed and contributed to six workshops for the mothers: 'Getting to know each other', 'Singing nursery rhymes', 'Noise-makers and listening', 'Talking with baby', 'Listening and looking out of doors' and 'Reviewing what we have done'.

The workshops were planned in detail, but the delivery was deceptively relaxed and informal. Ivy and her colleagues from other agencies understood the importance of modelling 'motherese' and were not afraid to muck-in to demonstrate how to play with babies. The workshops were scheduled one morning a week for six weeks for two hours. This allowed time for a cup of coffee and a snack for the babies and some relaxed chat as well as the workshop 'proper'. The mothers were cautious at first and attendance at the workshops was erratic. Nevertheless, Ivy kept the workshops running as planned. She videotaped some of the later sessions when everyone had learned to have fun without feeling inhibited. When Ivy shared the video extracts with the rest of the project team later, it was wonderful to see the gradual unfreezing of the mothers' tense faces and stiff bodies as they learned to enjoy the communication games with their babies.

Ivy encouraged the mothers to use the instant camera provided in the centre to record what they did at the workshops and stick the photographs into a scrapbook made out of a simple lined exercise book. These exercise books became significant objects for the mothers. We were allowed to borrow them for the project only on the promise that they would be returned to them in pristine condition. For once in their lives the ability of these women to 'mother' was being validated instead of questioned. The evidence of their growing confidence in communicating with their babies was captured in the video extracts and the notes they entered alongside the photos in their exercise books. This evidence made a strong impact on the whole project team. It was profound in its ordinariness.

Ivy began to pull together the insights she had gained into curriculum guidelines for speaking and listening with babies. Her notes formed the basis of a chart, to which many others in the project eventually contributed, showing how principles in supporting young children's learning in literacy can be translated into practice (see Table 6.1).

Underpinning these principles was the recurrent theme of paying due attention to the affective responses of adults and children in institutional settings and at home. Practitioners have always understood the power of emotions in learning, but researchers have been slow to investigate this most complex of fields. As Kress (1997: 110) pointed out, 'At the moment we know little about all of this: and we know very little because the issue is not quite respectable on the public agenda'. Ivy knew that a

Table 6.1   Principles of practice in supporting literacy learning

What we are looking for in children	What adults can do
0–12 months speaking and listening	
• Make simple sounds	• Model and repeat sounds
• Experiment with tongues, mouths, facial muscles, smile and laugh	• 'Play' with facial expressions, mouth and tongue movements, smile and laugh
• Make and sustain eye contact	• Make and sustain meaningful eye contact
• Wait for, respond to the physical behaviours of other children and adults	• Model/reinforce games involving physical movements (e.g. peekaboo)
• Take turns	• Encourage and exchange pauses, sounds in turn-taking
	• Sing to children
• Listen to, anticipate, predict sounds	• Model the rhythms, pitches, intonations of speech and musical sequences of sound
• Show pleasure in communicating	• Share fun/humour in play with babies
	• Develop close emotional/physical bonds with babies
• Repeat/mimic rhythms, sounds, singing	• Demonstrate animation, drama, play with words and sounds
• Know that there are different languages	• Value bilingualism for babies
	• Be consistent in feedback
• Respond to emotional warmth	• Have authentic emotional involvement with babies
'Book'/reading behaviours	
• Recognize books as source of fun and comfort	• Share books with babies
• Show interest in particular books	• Follow children's preferences for books
• Recognize and respond to visual information in images/ illustrations	• Draw children's attention to pictures
• Hold books, turn pages, make sounds, point to pictures	• Demonstrate book behaviour
• Listen to sounds and words of adults as they 'read' texts	• Emphasize key words and sounds by repetition or intonation
• Pay attention to magazines and catalogues	• Provide quiet quality times for children to 'browse' texts
• Watch videos/TV programmes attentively	• Sit with children and enjoy children's programmes
Mark-making	
• Observe older children mark-making with crayons, felt-tips etc.	• Ensure times for mixed-age group play

Table 6.1   (cont'd)

What we are looking for in children	What adults can do
• Pattern with limbs, hands, feet	• Provide time for physical exploration on a variety of surfaces, in a variety of postures
• Manipulate, control hands and fingers when exploring objects	• Provide safe play with a variety of natural and man made objects
• Pattern with food and drink	• Encourage children to enjoy sensuality of food/feeding
• Grasp crayons/pencils/brushes	• Provide some safe mark-making tools

12–24 months ALL THIS AND: speaking and listening

• Repeat sounds as 'words' in meaningful contexts	• Recognize, respond to, reinforce and extend first 'words'
• Respond to questions	
• Combine words to make units of meaning (e.g. 'dog gone', 'all gone', 'shoe gone')	• Positively promote bilingualism
	• Stress key 'content' words around daily routines: family comings and goings, food, bedtimes, TV programmes, animals
• Operate in more than one language	• Ask purposeful question
• Experiment with the intonation of questions and statements	• Demonstrate, exaggerate intonation patterns in dialogue with toddlers/ babies
• 'Sing song' to well-known nursery rhymes and songs	• Sing with and for children
• Mimic actions/rhythms of songs and rhymes	• Model actions and rhythms of songs and rhymes
• Listen to music	• Model listening to music
• Recognize 'function' sounds (e.g. telephone, washing machine, ambulance and police sirens)	• Respond to key signature jingles/tunes (e.g. soaps, news ads.)
	• Draw attention to everyday 'function' sounds
• Respond to adult prompts	• Talk to children frequently alongside daily routines
• Have a large 'passive' vocabulary	• Repeat 'instruction' in meaningful contexts (e.g. 'wave/say bye bye')
• Have a meaningful 'dialogue' with others	• 'Tune into' children's initiatives to communicate (often non-verbal) and respond

Book behaviour

• Listen to a story	• Read stories as often as possible
• Select a favourite book	• Tune into children's preferences
	• Encourage children to make choices
• Recognize images/photos of familiar events and people	• Point out images of and talk about key shared experiences/significant people in children's lives

Table 6.1   (cont'd)

What we are looking for in children	What adults can do
• Predict repetitive texts	• Play with repetition, fun with well-known stories
• Recognize significant food labels/symbols	• Talk about labels/symbols on packaging

Mark-making

• Experiment with mark-making indoors and outdoors with a range of media	• Provide a range of safe resources for mark-making indoors (e.g. crayons, paint, clay, Playdough) and outdoors (e.g. water, sticks, mud, pebbles)
• Intensely watch older children and adults mark-making, drawing and writing	• Model mark-making for communication
• Control mark-making	• Set up mark-making opportunities, especially involving mixed age groups
• Press keys on computers	• Provide access to IT

24–36 months ALL THIS AND: speaking and listening

• Form new sentences	• Extend and model novel sentences
• Ask questions	• Give positive feedback
	• Reply to questions
• Demonstrate grasp of language 'rules'	• Repeat back inappropriate language in appropriate form but with sensitivity
• Reproduce language heard all around them in 'real' contexts	• Provide opportunities for children to access many kinds of language use (e.g. from videos, shops, parties, community and family events)
• Have a conversation	• Provide role play areas and equipment and toys for children to represent speech and behaviours in role
• Use language to make connections	• Talk about past, present and future shared experiences with children
• Communicate in more than one language	• Offer access to a range of languages

Reading/book behaviour

• 'Pretend' read	• Share books and storytelling
• 'Tell' a narrative	• Explore everyday literacies of home communities
	• Extend children's interests to wider cultural literacies (e.g. books, signs and symbols, pictures, moving images)
• Concentrate on a sustained story in words, pictures, moving image forms	• Introduce vocabulary and link with printed form in functional literacy books, and from screens (TV and Internet).

Table 6.1   (cont'd)

What we are looking for in children	What adults can do
• Create/invent playing with words rhymes and jokes • Recognize some letters and numerals in 'real' contexts	• Introduce children to libraries • Encourage a playful approach to using words and telling stories • Introduce children to letters and numerals in authentic contexts and where appropriate in more than one language

36–60 months ALL THIS AND: speaking and listening

• Use an extensive vocabulary • Make complex sentences • Predict what might happen • Argue with adults • Consciously use different 'voices' for different purposes • Make up own stories • Sing and make music	• Model and introduce new vocabulary • Do not speak down to children, but match language to appropriate level • Provide/structure a wide range of real life and play experiences • Model/expose children to a range of language registers • Have fun with language • Model singing and both making and listening to different kinds of music

Book behaviour/reading

• Begin to 'read like a book' and then to want to learn to read • Watch videos/TV programmes with sustained attention • Recognize letters and words in print • Decode a range of signs and symbols	• Encourage an interest in learning to read • Provide access to a wide range of types of books, catalogues, magazines etc. • Talk about and watch favourite video/TV programmes • Draw attention to print/signs/symbols all around

Mark-making

• Gain increasing control of mark-making tools/media to represent ideas and communicate them to others • Write and draw intentional messages	• Diversify 'authentic' experiences of real life mark-making as models • Provide access to range of media • Pay serious attention to children's drawings and emergent writing and respond to their messages

lack of sound, affective communication between babies and adults was a danger for her own staff as well as for the children's mothers. Her gut feeling is borne out by research evidence.

Peter Elfer and Dorothy Selleck are in their third and final year of research into the care and educational needs of children under 3 in nurseries. Their findings emphasize the importance, during what we called in Chapter 4 (see page 64) the 'intersubjective phase' of children's development, of key adults forming authentic emotional relationships with the children in their care. These authentic emotional relationships are reflected in the quality of speech interactions between adults and children (Wells 1985) and in their participation in joint involvement episodes (Schaffer 1992). Hopefully their 'conversations' with babies will involve them in the dynamic kind of language formats (Bruner 1983) also discussed in Chapter 4. Sadly, the data from Selleck and Elfer, based on analysis of 150 hours of observations of babies in 15 nurseries indicate that where organizational systems allocate care workers to attend to the needs of too many babies, workers are driven to depersonalize their relationships with them. They concentrate on the 'presenting' needs of the babies for whom they are responsible – feeding, cleaning and changing them. It seems that it is not humanly possible for them to form close emotional relationships with so many young children without suffering from emotional overload; so they have to retreat to the safer areas of caring for the children's physical needs. In the hustle and bustle of getting through the daily tasks involved in the physical care of the children for whom they are responsible, staff are not able to use the kind of enriching, affectionate talk around these routines which, Bruner argued, forms the basis of babies' learning about 'conversations'.

Learning to love books

While Ivy focused on speaking and listening, Jenny was interested in the effects of introducing babies to books. She was influenced by the work of Barry Wade (1993) in the Bookstart Scheme who monitored the impact of giving books to babies and supporting their parents in story reading skills. His seminal work is now being extended nationally by the Book Trust (Book Trust 1998).

Jenny's professional role was to support family literacy in a local authority funded project. She based her action research cycles on work with mother and toddler groups meeting in primary schools, clinics or community centres. Over 40 parents/carers were contacted via health visitors and given a 'bookbag' when their babies were 7 months old. The bookbag contained: a board book, some simple advice about books, a library joining card and times of the local library sessions, a song and rhyme booklet, a poster and a bookmark. The pack also included an invitation for parents to join a series of workshops to help their babies' literacy development. A third of those contacted took up the offer of attending the workshops. They were from a wide range of socioeconomic and educational backgrounds. The only thing they had in common was a baby aged 7 months!

Each workshop, held once a fortnight, had a focus but, as with Ivy's work with parents, allowed time for socialization. For many isolated parents, the chance to socialize during the day was a very important benefit of attending the workshops. There was always a crèche worker to help look after the babies; but mostly they just clambered around amongst the adults. Jenny was the first to admit that some of her workshops worked better than others:

> Indeed, the occasional session was chaotic as I tried, unsuccessfully, to compete with up to twelve extremely vocal and mobile babies! However, we had a lot of fun at the sessions too.

The content of the workshops was geared around the needs and ideas of each particular group of parents/carers, but a typical menu would be: how to share books with babies; choosing books for babies; songs and rhymes; making books; early language development; promoting literacy skills at home; drawing and writing; learning to read; encouraging speaking and listening skills; television. There were always plenty of books around for the babies and adults to enjoy together, and the opportunity to take a book home for the fortnight. Parents were asked to notice which books their babies liked best – the format (board or cloth), the layout (with text or without; photos or illustrations), and the content (stories they enjoyed). Jenny was fascinated to observe the definite preferences of the babies for types of books or for particular transitory favourites. Their likes and dislikes seemed to be based on a combination of features – preferences for the feel of board books or cloth books, the impact of photo illustrations rather than drawings, the connections images made with important objects in their own lives, the kinds of fun interactions the books induced in their parents/carers. She observed that the babies quickly learned how to hold the books and turn the pages once book behaviours had been modelled by the adults sharing books with them and were capable of concentrating on books for short periods on their own.

Using the knowledge they had gained of what their babies most enjoyed, the parents/carers were given the opportunity to choose a second book for their babies when they reached 12 months.

Jenny's notes identified changes in the parents' behaviours too:

> It was pleasing to observe the parents' surprise and joy at what, with a little encouragement from them, their babies were actually achieving. For the majority of parents this was like an awakening. 'I

didn't know my baby would be able to do this. What else can she do?' From the original impetus of the workshops, groups of parents are continuing to meet to look at how babies develop through play. The parents are 'hooked'. They also enjoyed the social side of meeting. Role modelling of parenting skills within the groups has had a strong impact. It has made me review the way I work to 'spread the word' about the development of literacy in babies.

In her evaluation of her work for the project, Jenny noted:

Observing the literacy behaviour of both the parents and their babies was a fascinating and very satisfying experience as I watched the changes in both. The really exciting thing was that we, the parents and I, actually saw the babies taking a keen interest in, and responding enthusiastically to, books. As the parents became more confident, the parent/baby interaction around the books blossomed and we saw a love of books being fostered in the babies.

We will return to a more detailed discussion about the key principles of involving parents in young children's development and learning in Chapter 9.

   18 months to 3 years

Mark-making

Val has a teaching background. At the time of the project she was employed on a local authority Single Regeneration Budget-funded scheme with the dual aims of helping parents/carers to learn more about their children's education while at the same time encouraging them to further their own learning through training or employment opportunities. She was supporting a literacy programme through a weekly parent and toddler club which had been running for two and a half years in a classroom at a primary school.

She noticed that there were less opportunities for the toddlers to explore mark-making than other aspects of literacy. Each week pencils, crayons and paper were set out on a table, but she noted that the children spent little time there, and parents even less. She decided to make mark-making, drawing and emergent writing the focus of her research. She began to read around the subject and noted in her diary:

Although I had worked within an early years framework for over ten years, when I carried out a literature search and review of emergent writing there was still a lot I didn't know and needed to find out. I was not an expert.

Val planned a sequence of activities with a specific focus each week on strategies to encourage mark-making and writing skills. The target areas were listed as: hand-eye coordination, fine motor control, experimenting with a range of media, teaching the vocabulary of drawing and emergent writing, and extending children's learning.

Once she got going she observed that while she was seated at the table children came willingly to join in with the activities, appeared to enjoy them and were making progress in the skills targeted. But despite her years of experience as a teacher, she confessed that she found it a challenge to judge exactly when to extend, challenge or direct such young children's mark-making. Entries from her diary show just how much the children, aged from 11 to 36 months, were learning about drawing and writing:

> Ellie, aged 11 months, moved towards the crayons, picked them up and began to explore them one by one with her mouth. She watched what the other children were doing, moved away but came back to the table several more times.

> Damien, aged 2 years and 4 months, indicated that he wanted to use the pencil I was holding to draw. He said, 'Pencil draw'. I offered him a variety of pencils and chubby crayons from the pot. Damien chose the pencils. He made several spiral patterns.

> Katy, aged 2 years and 11 months, had good pencil control. She drew me a number of star shapes and a travelling zigzag pattern. I chatted with her about what she was doing and she repeated that she had drawn a zigzag picture. I was making notes and Katy asked me what I was doing. I explained that I was writing about her drawing. She asked me why and I said that I thought that it was interesting and that she was good at drawing. She asked me to write her name, first on my page and then on her piece of paper. She made some marks on her paper, pushed it across to show me and told me she'd written her name.

> Alice, aged 3 years, drew several rectangular shapes on her paper and told me they were fences. She also made several marks and then began to copy letters in her name – A and C. The letters were well formed and she managed to match them accurately to the letters I'd written. I praised her and pointed out the similarities between other marks she'd been making and the letters in her name.

In her research diary Val noted that she believed that the parents were not engaging with what she was doing with the children on the mark-making table. She wrote:

At first I thought I had created a cocoon around children's learning and essentially left parents outside it. However, closer observations revealed that many of the parents were listening and observing the interactions that were taking place.

She then made the strategic decision to mount a display of the children's mark-making and emergent writing for the parents on the board in the classroom where the parent and toddler club met. She was staggered by its impact on the parents:

The display became an amazing tool through which to discuss the children's writing/drawing development. I pointed out to them recurring patterns, movements or the beginning of letter shapes, representational drawings or invented writing.

In Bruner's (1996) terms the display board became a cultural tool around which a series of interactions between the children, their parents and the practitioners, situated in the context of the parent and toddler club workshops, focused on the children's understanding of how to make meanings in drawing and writing (see Chapter 4 for discussion about the way in which children are inducted to be competent users of the cultural tools of society). However, there were too many drawing/writing examples being generated to display them all, so Val suggested that each parent might like to use an exercise book to mount and display their own children's work as a way of monitoring their progress over the weeks. The parents brought in photographs of the children to stick on the front of the exercise books. The books became a focus for the parent and child to review what they had been doing each week as they stuck in their drawings and mark-making. Once again a simple exercise book became a cultural tool in the process of creating shared understandings between parents and professionals. Val noted in her research diary:

The eagerness of the parents to stick the children's work into the books and record their descriptions of how they'd been arrived at really took me by surprise.

The parents began to understand the subtlety and power of young children's mark-making. One parent remarked to Val, 'I used to think it was just scribbling'.

For the next step of her research, Val decided to move on to encouraging parents and children to make connections between their own mark-making and written communication in the real world. She knew that the local post office was a regular port of call for parents on their way to and from the school. She asked the parents to lift the children up when they next visited the post office so that they could see what was going on over the counter. She encouraged them to talk to the children during the week about writing and posting letters, paying bills, buying stamps, weighing parcels, cashing giros etc. At the next workshop session she launched the idea of making a role play area for the children based on the post office. Over the next few weeks the parents collected resources – junk mail, postcards, envelopes, stamps, forms, greetings cards – and made equipment – a post box and a counter – for the toddlers' post office. Parents were relaxed about joining the children in the role play where the stimulus for talk and play was a real shared experience. Adults and children wrote, drew, filled in forms, talked about symbols and logos and filled in lottery tickets together. One of the children persuaded her mother to set up a sub-post office at home!

Several of the parents began to notice how closely the children watched when they were writing. One said to Val, 'He often wants to write himself now when he sees me writing'. Adults were drawn quite naturally into extending the children's knowledge base without recourse to mimicking didactic teaching styles. It was suddenly OK for parents and children to write and draw together companionably in joint involvement episodes with both adults and children paying respectful attention to each other's meaning making. Val noted one parent carefully explaining the concept of a prepaid envelope to her 3-year-old.

In her evaluation of what she had learned from her research, Val wrote:

> We learnt how important it was to tune into and discuss with children their drawings and emergent writing as they were doing it and to encourage further efforts by giving feedback and showing real interest in their mark-making.

Kress (1997: 17) made the same important point about paying serious attention to children's mark-making:

> The child's written signs are the effect of their meaning-making actions, arising out of their interest, using what they have available as representational means . . . The signs which children make are, despite their differences from adult form, fully meaningful in every sense. The child's actions have to be understood as productive and transformative of their own representational resources, as well as those of the community around them.

For Val, another important self-realization was that by adopting the 'school' behaviours of sitting and 'teaching' children at the 'work table' she had inadvertently excluded the parents from engaging with their children. Once she had demystified 'the mark-making table' by letting parents into the magic circle of 'teacher' knowledge by literally 'displaying' it to them on the notice board, and interpreting that explanation in terms that made sense to her audience, they became hooked on their own personal journeys of discovery about the meanings their own children were making in marks.

It is this kind of approach that makes the philosophy of the famous Reggio Emilia pre-school centres so compelling (Edwards *et al.* 1993). Pedagogues, practitioners, parents and children are engaged together in exploring the many languages children use to express their ideas and communicate their meaning making to others. Malaguzzi (1987), the founding father of the Reggio Emilia pre-school innovation, argued that 'our image of the child should be of one that is rich in potential, strong, powerful, competent and most of all connected to adults and other children'. In this example of a reflective practioner at work, children, practitioners and parents were empowered by acknowledging the central role of learning associated with the language of their everyday lives within their knowledge community. Most importantly, children, parents and professionals were learning from and about each other.

3 to 5 years

From 2- to 3-D representation and back again

Molly was the manager of an inner-city early years centre. The staff had been working for some time to enhance the quality of mark-making across all areas of the curriculum, but they had noticed that it was rare to observe children's mark-making being connected to play in the construction area. They had also observed that the range of children regularly using the construction area during free-flow times in the mornings was limited. Boys dominated construction play. Access in the afternoons was restricted by the fact that the resources were housed in a 'family base' where children were based with their keyworker.

Molly identified the focus of her action research cycle as the promotion of meaning making in construction play for the 3- to 5-year-olds. Her aims were: to increase access to construction play for more children; to encourage the use of mark-making in the construction area; to improve the quality of interactions between adults and children in the construction area; to extend children's learning through 2-D representations and 3-D models in meaning making.

Molly set out an action plan which involved the staff recording their own observations of activities in the construction area in an agreed format. The format was a simple chart with spaces to record the name, gender and age of the child observed; other children with whom they played; whether an adult was involved; what the children did; language used and any evidence of mark-making in general or specifically related to construction activities. The first sets of observations were gathered during the month of October. Molly and her deputy also made some observations in the area. Molly noted that though the staff were slightly uncomfortable at first about being observed they quickly forgot she was there.

When the first set of staff observations were analysed and the results shared at a staff meeting several key issues were raised. The most usual number of children working together was three. Boys represented two thirds of the children using the area. In half of the observations children were not talking. One third of the observations showed children using mark-making, but only 5 per cent of these were linked to construction play. It tended to be the same children who regularly played in the area.

However, the analysis of activities observed when Molly and her deputy were observing the area later in the month showed quite different patterns. In these, the girls represented two thirds and the boys one third of those actively involved in construction play. Language and mark-making related to construction was much more apparent. As Molly ruefully observed, the effect of the managers' presence in the area clearly had a dramatic impact on how the practitioners structured their own and the children's participation!

As the project progressed it became clear that the staff were unsure about how to get the best out of meaning making through construction play. Molly set up a series of visits to other pre-school settings for staff to observe the quality of their construction activities. She invited one of the researchers to give an input at a staff meeting followed by a workshop for staff to explore the possibilities for themselves of construction materials (Community Playthings, Duplo, Mobilo, H. Blocks and Stickle Bricks) and small figure play. In a second session they were encouraged to use drawing or writing to extend their thinking. Staff were asked to use these experiences as the basis for planning a series of activities for the children.

In December the staff and Molly set about a second set of observations in the construction area to monitor for any changes. For Molly there were some disappointments: boys still dominated two thirds of the activities and there was evidence that the same rather limited range of children were playing in the area. However, there was a dramatic increase in the amount of mark-making related to the construction play to 85 per cent of the incidents. Overall, children used mark-making in the area for two thirds of the time they were observed.

A typical observation involved the follow-up activity of the story of *Goldilocks and the Three Bears*. In the construction area the staff had collected together several copies of the story, Community Plaything blocks, paper, card, scissors, glue sticks and felt-tip pens. The observation recorded how the children moved fluently backwards and forwards between making the chairs, tables and beds out of the blocks and role playing the story, taking turns to play the main characters; drawing out props such as the porridge bowls and spoons on big sheets of paper and cutting them out to use in play episodes; and then making small pictures of the bears and Goldilocks on the card and cutting them out to play a second version of the story in miniature. Finally, these second-level representations were stuck together with sellotape onto a base board cut from an old cardboard box to recreate the story scene in an elaborate and detailed model. Molly noted in her diary:

> The adults learned how children have the ability to recall from a previous day and transfer a story into representations in the construction area taking one step further each time. They also learned that children are good role models for each other in sparking off ideas about expressing themselves in speech, 3-D models and 2-D drawings.

Molly's project was a wonderful example of Kress's (1997) multimodal representations, and of children using Bruner's (1996) enactive and iconic representations. With its emphasis on both language and mathematical thinking, it is a good point at which to move on to the chapters on how young children learn to become mathematicians.

 ## Suggested reading

For prompts for nursery rhymes and action songs, Matterson, E. (1969) *This Little Puffin: Finger Play and Nursery Rhymes* (London: Puffin) is a good collection. Raymond Briggs' *The Mother Goose Treasury* (1969), published by Hamish Hamilton and Puffin is a good anthology of nursery rhymes. The Opies' *Children's Games in Street and Playground*, published by Oxford University Press in 1969 is a useful source of information on traditional street and playground games.

Further reading on the emotional aspects of learning includes Shaw, J. (1995) *Education, Gender and Anxiety* (London: Taylor & Francis); Salzberger-Wittenberg, I., Henry, G. and Osborne, E. (1983) *The Emotional Experience of Learning and Teaching* (London: Routledge); and Golman, D. (1996) *Emotional Intelligence* (London: Bloomsbury).

Leila Berg's (1977) *Reading and Loving*, published by Routledge & Kegan Paul, is a classic. She describes the warmth and sensuous delights of young children sharing the enjoyment of learning to read with caring adults.

7 Mathematical learning

 Becoming a numerate person

Is being numerate simply a question of being good with numbers? The 1982 Cockcroft Report, which has had an enormous influence on mathematics education, suggests that being numerate implies:

> the possession of two attributes. The first is an 'at-homeness' with numbers and an ability to cope with the practical mathematical demands of everyday life. The second is an ability to have some appreciation and understanding of information which is presented in mathematical terms, for instance in graphs, charts or tables ... a numerate person should be able to appreciate and understand some of the ways in which mathematics can be used as a means of communication.
>
> (Cockcroft 1982: para. 34)

Being numerate, therefore, is more than a recognition of numbers, is closely linked to mathematical understandings and serves two purposes. First, numeracy is useful in everyday life and second, it allows us to think mathematically in specifically mathematical contexts.

'At-homeness' with numbers is certainly important. Research over the last two decades has been telling us that familiarity with numbers and their uses helps children to think mathematically (Nunes and Bryant 1996). This may seem so obvious that it is not worth mentioning. However, so strong has been the influence of Piaget and his concern with children learning through action rather than through language, that pre-school provision has often emphasized sorting and matching at the expense of number. Munn and Schaffer (1993), for example, in their detailed study of literacy and numeracy interactions in Strathclyde nurseries in the early 1990s found a surprisingly low level of numeracy-based interactions between children and adults.

Our research partnership worked with the messages from research about the need to offer a developmentally sound set of experiences to children to support early numeracy slowly and carefully, and to provide opportunities for children to use their developing mathematical understandings. Our thinking about children and mathematics took us, usually simultaneously, to three focuses: young children as mathematical thinkers, how adults support children's mathematical thinking and the mathematical experiences that can be provided in pre-school settings. In this chapter we shall look at young children as mathematical thinkers. In the next chapter we shall examine how pre-school provision can support children's mathematical thinking and will illustrate the discussion with examples of provision from the partnership.

   ## Young children as mathematical thinkers

Being able to think mathematically

Children learn a great deal about aspects of mathematics before they start formal school (Aubrey 1996). They therefore enter school with a great deal of knowledge on which teachers can build. But then something seems to go wrong. Very few students specialize in mathematics beyond A level and a large number leave school disliking mathematics. Current thinking suggests that the problem lies in seeing mathematics as a set of formal principles that are learnt as abstract knowledge and then applied in the world. People are simply not very good at applying abstract principles to real life situations.

As a result, efforts have been made to ensure that we help children to learn mathematical principles in situations that are as near to real life as possible (De Corte *et al.* 1996). The rationale is that when they deal with real life mathematical problems children learn mathematical principles, develop a disposition to engage with mathematics and learn useful mathematics which they can use in both everyday life and in more formal mathematics situations. Pre-school provision is well placed to work with this view of mathematics as situated in real life settings, as thankfully it is not constrained by a history of mathematics teaching which emphasizes abstract problem solving. In pre-school provision children can gradually learn to operate mathematically in situations which are part of their general exploration of their worlds.

However, in order to be able to operate mathematically in an activity a child needs to recognize the mathematics in the experience, be able to think logically about the response and have the strategies available to be able to respond. Children's understanding of basic logical concepts is therefore central to how they see, interpret and respond to activities that can be tackled mathematically. We can't do justice here to Piaget's work on children's logico-mathematical thought and the frameworks which have drawn on it (see, for example, Campbell and Olson 1990; Meadows 1993). Equally, however, we cannot discuss pre-school mathematics without mentioning *conservation*.

Conservation of quantity in Piaget's writings refers to a child's capacity to know that the quantity remains the same even though its shape may be changed. For example, conservation of continuous quantity is achieved when children recognize that when a ball of Plasticine is rolled into a sausage or when the water from a squat beaker is poured into a tall one, the quantities in each case are not changed. *Conservation of number* is evident when children can tell that a set of objects – for example, five sweets – remains a set of five sweets whether they are arrayed in a line or in a circle. Conservation of number is particularly important for the development of numeracy as we shall see when we discuss cardinal numbers in a moment.

Children's mathematical development is therefore a complex interplay between how they interpret their worlds and how they are able to respond to what they understand. The challenge that their mathematical learning presents to early educators is perhaps greater than children's literacy development because the mathematics in children's worlds is less obviously evident to them. We therefore need to think carefully about how we elicit the mathematics in children's experiences and give them the wherewithal to deal with it. We do know that an understanding of number helps children to respond mathematically so we shall make this our first focus.

The development of children's understanding of number

In Chapter 4 we suggested that adults should think aloud so that children can begin to glimpse how they see, interpret and respond to the world. Children can then appropriate adults' responses. Let's listen to a mother thinking aloud while waiting for a number Seven bus with her 4-year-old: 'Oh dear that's the third Fifty Three in the last five minutes! Even if a Seven comes now we'll be a couple of minutes late. Oh here it is! Have you got your two ten pences ready?'

The mother's talk is rich in number but it also tells us just how difficult it is to understand numbers. She has used number in a variety of ways: to *denote* (i.e. 'a [number] Seven'); to *order* (i.e. 'the third'); and to indicate a *number in a set* (i.e. 'two'). This is without the complications of large numbers, time, money and alternative language such as 'a couple'. Children may appropriate the language – that is, learn language formats such as 'one for you and one for me' or 'none left' – but do not so quickly grasp the meanings. Learning to use the language of number and to become numerate is a complex process and *takes a very long time*.

Children are immersed in numerical experiences in their daily lives whether they are being persuaded to eat 'one more' spoonful of yoghurt or having their feet measured for shoes. However, it is clear that even though young children can respond to these activities in conversations with adults, they do not understand the numbers involved in the same ways that adults do. This lack of understanding is hardly surprising when we consider the different ways that numbers are used. Fuson and Hall (1983) suggest that young children meet number words in at least six different contexts and in each they serve a slightly different purpose:

1 In the *sequence context*, strings of numbers are produced in the conventional order but there is no intention to count objects. For example, 'One, two, three, four, five. Once I caught a fish alive'. Or, 'Close your eyes and count to ten'.
2 In the *counting context*, numbers are applied to objects. For example, by pointing to or touching objects as they are counted.
3 In the *cardinal context*, numbers represent what Fuson and Hall describe as the 'manyness' or numerosity of a set of objects. The ability to use number in this way comes gradually – for example, children understand 'two' quite early through familiarity with two shoes, two gloves etc. Young children also learn, through stories, that there are three bears and three Billy Goats Gruff. But recognizing the cardinal qualities of a number – that is, actually understanding that the last number you say when counting a set of objects represents the number of objects in the set, comes relatively slowly and depends on a child's capacity to *conserve* numbers.
4 In the *measure context*, number words represent the manyness or numerosity of the units of measurement used. In the construction area in Alison's nursery Connor demonstrated his early gropings towards understanding linear measurement when, after applying the tape measure to his boat, he told Alison that it measured '150,000 pounds'.
5 In the *ordinal context*, a number word represents the relative position, size or other measurable of an object in a group of objects (the third bus to pass the stop, the second tallest person in the group or the fourth child in the family).
6 In the *nonnumerical context*, number words are simply names – for example, a number Seven bus, the number of your house, a telephone number. Fuson and Hall suggest that too much attention to nonnumerical

numbers might inhibit children's understandings of the other qualities of numbers.

In addition to distinguishing the different uses of numbers in different contexts children need to understand some basic principles about counting before they can be said to be able to count. Gelman and Gallistel (1986) identified five such principles:

1 The *one-to-one principle* requires children to be able to match the counting words to the items to be counted.
2 The *stable order principle* refers to children's ability to repeat counting words in the correct order. This is particularly demanding in the English language which has less of a stable pattern in its number words compared with some other languages. Children therefore need to learn number sequences by rote in the first instance.
3 The *cardinal principle* has already been described. Grasping this principle is central to a child's capacity to add or subtract.
4 The *abstraction principle* alerts us to the fact that children do not need to count sets of similar objects in order to use cardinal numbers. That is, they do not need to count four cups to label the collection as a set of four. They will, for example, be able to label sets of 'things on the table' as four 'things'.
5 The *order irrelevance principle* is evident when children can happily start to count a set of objects from any point in the set. That is, they are recognizing that an object is not a 'one' but that numbers are used simply to count and not to label individual objects.

The interplay between first recognizing the mathematics in a situation and then using and developing mathematical responses is quite messy. Saxe *et al.* explored the relationship between numerical 'function' (what numbers are used for – e.g. indicating the total number in a set, comparing sets) and the 'forms' of numerical activity undertaken by young children (the strategies children use when they tackle a mathematical function – e.g. counting, one-to-one matching). As part of their study of parents, children between the ages of 30 and 60 months and numeracy, they came up with a developmental sequence showing the relationship between the mathematics in an activity and the strategies children use to deal with number experiences. The sequence has four levels with level one as the least complex (Saxe *et al.* 1987: 8–12). We have illustrated their sequence with our own examples, as follows.

At *Level 1*, children use number words without making a lasting one-to-one match between a word and an object. They will produce a sequence of numbers, though not necessarily in the correct order and will not appear to use numbers to represent the manyness or cardinal aspect of a set of objects. For example, when faced with five sweets to count children may point vaguely and say one, two, three, six, eight. Or, having counted the sweets correctly to five, they will recount when asked how many sweets there are.

At *Level 2*, children can match a number to an object and can therefore count objects. Furthermore, they recognize that the last number they said represents the number of objects in the set they have counted. For example, having counted the five sweets in front of them they can tell you that there are five sweets on the table – that is, they can *conserve* numbers and use them as cardinal numbers.

At *Level 3*, children can compare two groups of numbers and can reproduce a second set of numbers. But they do so by using the counting strategies they used at Level 2. For example, they will compare two sets of sweets by one-to-one matching. They will not count to five and then to four and say that the first set has one more sweet.

At *Level 4*, children begin to use arithmetic strategies. For example, when asked to add two sets of numbers they will start with the cardinal number of the first set (five sweets) and count on the four in the second set as six, seven, eight, nine.

Children's understanding of number seems to develop slowly and build on previous experiences. Even babies appear to recognize the difference between sets of two and of three objects (Baroody 1987) and 2-year-olds start to string together number sequences even though they may not be counting as they do so. It is also clear from the four levels just outlined that as children move through the levels of competence they build directly on their achievements at the previous level. Saxe *et al.* (1987) suggested that children pass through these levels aided by adults who help them to use their existing numerical skills to tackle slightly more complex problems and develop new understandings. For example, once a child understands that if four people are to sit at the table four places need to be set (a Level 2 understanding), she or he can be encouraged to collect sets of four forks, knives, plates etc. (leading to a Level 3 understanding). Importantly, children tackle these problems in activities that are embedded, often playfully, in conversations and games. These conversations and games provide children with familiar language and action formats which enable them to safely explore the mathematical challenges that are offered.

The distinction outlined by Saxe *et al.* (1987) between mathematical demands in an activity and the strategies that children bring to bear on them is helpful for two reasons. First, it tells us that adults can help children identify the potential mathematics in an activity. Second, it reminds us to build on children's current strategies when first tackling a new mathematical experience. We shall look at the roles of adults later in this chapter and focus here on children's number strategies.

It is clear from the outlines of number contexts and uses we have given, that children's abilities to reproduce number words tells us very little about how they understand number and what it is that they believe numbers are and do. Penny Munn's interviews and assessments with 4-year-old children in Strathclyde nurseries in the year before formal schooling revealed that although the children were able to sequence numbers very well, they had little sense of number as a way of quantifying – rather, they saw it as something playful (Munn 1997a). Munn suggests that although the children appeared to be counting they were not doing so as a mathematical activity but as an imitative activity. We have already suggested in Chapter 4 that imitation of behaviour and appropriation of language are important features of learning. However, they are not the same as mastery, and Munn's observations remind us of the need for careful assessment before moving children on to more demanding number activities.

Clearly, children's early familiarity with number words and how they are used appears to be beneficial. If using numbers is associated with fun and achievement in playful number activities children are being helped to acquire a disposition to deal with numbers and sets of behaviours, such as pointing and sequencing, that will give them confidence. Also, once children have some number vocabulary they can use it when exploring patterns, sorting shapes, weighing objects or assessing capacity, and therefore more widely interpret and respond to the mathematics around them.

Importantly, a developing understanding of number and its uses leads children towards the recording of their experiences through mark-making, which gradually becomes more systematic and again assists their mathematical thinking.

Learning to record

Cockcroft's (1982) definition of being numerate given at the beginning of this chapter describes mathematics as a means of communication. We would argue that being able to communicate mathematically is valuable in both daily life and in specifically mathematical contexts such as formal schooling. Sometimes that communication is with others and sometimes with ourselves when we make mathematical records in order to assist our own problem solving.

However, in order to communicate mathematically, young learners need first to recognize that there is a connection between the mark that they make and what it stands for – for example, that one splodge in a circle stands for one person at the tea table. Only gradually will young children learn to convert their own private and situation-specific system of signs into a system that is context-free and easily understood by others. The first step, that a mark represents a quantity, is therefore important. But all that we have said about number suggests that this ability is quite an achievement for a young child and appears to develop

Figure 7.1   Children's recording strategies in number
Source: Munn (1994b).

gradually alongside a growing understanding of how numbers are used and of the publicly understood numeral system.

Munn (1994b) identified six ways in which children record numbers after 'counting' which seem to indicate children's developing ability to use numbers as symbols (that is, understanding that the numeral '4' represents a cardinal number). Children's recording strategies range from 'pretend writing' to 'conventionally used numerals' and are shown in Figure 7.1.

After monitoring the development in recording and the strategic use of number of 49 children in their final pre-school year, Munn (1997b) concluded that children's ability to read their own number records, regardless of whether these were recorded as numerals, seems to support and be supported by their developing understanding of number and its uses.

Munn's conclusions (1997b) about the relationships between children's strategies and their numerical thinking once again remind us of the complex relationship between use of numbers and mathematical understanding outlined by Saxe *et al.* (1987). One challenge to early educators arising from Munn's conclusions is: just how do we pace children's recording and ensure that children's representations of number assist them to use number? We cannot help children to understand what numbers are and do simply by training them to write the number symbols. For example, when Munn assessed the same children after one term of formal schooling (Munn 1997b), she found that seven of the children who had learnt to write numerals while at formal school were not referring to the numbers they had written to help them answer her questions. It seemed that they had learnt how to form the numerals but not how to use them strategically as numbers when faced with a mathematical activity.

Munn's work suggests that being able to use and understand numerals helps children once they need to be able to refer to their written records to support their mathematical problem solving. She therefore advises early years professionals to be alert to children's developing number 'literacy' (Munn 1997b). However, Munn's point about number literacy is a subtle but important one. She argues that developing number literacy cannot be seen as similar to emergent writing. This is because children's meaningful use of numerals depends on their understanding of the number concept being represented by the numeral – for example, that 'five' is being used in a particular situation as a cardinal number. Munn's analysis is supported by other researchers working in the field of young children's early mathematical learning (Baroody 1993). Preschool teachers therefore have to guard against introducing numerals too rapidly.

Before they achieve number literacy children can be helped by adults who talk to them about their alternative symbols in ways that encourage them to understand how their tallies or drawings do represent specific quantities and how these representations can act as records of their counting. These interactions should occur as part of open-ended activities which allow children to construct their own understandings of numbers and how they can be used so that they can move, over time, to use numbers when they record.

The range of mathematical experiences in pre-school provision

In this chapter we have focused largely on number. This is because it seems clear that a grasp of basic numeracy concepts helps children as they think and act as young mathematicians while operating in their worlds whether they are, for example, measuring, weighing or sorting. However, early mathematics is not simply a question of understanding numbers and how they are used. Mathematical activities include becoming familiar with shapes, learning to recognize patterns, working with ordering and sequencing, and planning and problem solving.

All of these experiences are easily incorporated into fun activities for children. For example, sequencing and pattern recognition can become part of printing or painting activities. Becoming familiar with shapes is often part of dance and song times, and, of course, cooking and eating. Sequencing is a central aspect of stories whether children listen or are encouraged to tell or act out their own short narratives. Ordering is experienced at meal times, in singing, and everyday turn-taking. Sorting and set making are often parts of tidy-up routines. Planning and problem solving can be encouraged in building and role play.

As we shall see in the next chapter our research partners were inventive in how they ensured that mathematical focuses could be found role play, imaginative games, songs and other familiar pre-school contexts. The children were able to engage with the mathematics, sometimes with the help of adults who modelled language and behaviour in conversations, and sometimes simply because the resources captured children's imaginations and led them to particular forms of behaviour. The most important element in all these activities was that the children developed confidence and saw whatever mathematics they experienced as fun.

 ## Building on children's everyday experiences of mathematics

We have stressed that children's experience in pre-school settings is not a question of simply preparing children for the school curriculum. Rather it is an opportunity to develop young children's cultural capital so that they enter school as keen learners with a strong sense of their own effectiveness and with some of the basic conceptual understandings on which more formal forms of schooling can build. Far more than schools, pre-school settings are able to work closely with parents and collaborate over the informal learning experiences that are part of the cultural capital provided at home.

As we have already seen in this chapter the informal learning and cultural capital provided at home in mathematics can be considerable. One of the challenges facing teachers in the first few years of formal schooling is how to translate informal understandings, which are sometimes of limited use in formal mathematics, into more accepted ways of thinking and acting mathematically. This challenge will not face many educare professionals, for in educare the emphasis has to be on developing and augmenting the everyday mathematical experiences of young children so that they familiarize themselves with mathematical concepts which are embedded in meaningful experiences.

The focus in pre-school mathematics is therefore a question of developing children's enthusiastic dispositions towards seeing the mathematics in situations and having the mathematical knowledge on which to draw in order to respond. The role of the assisting adult is therefore to sustain motivation, to help children see the mathematics and to offer some aids to organizing their responses, perhaps by modelling – for example, seeing patterns, sorting into sets, or using cardinal numbers when describing sets.

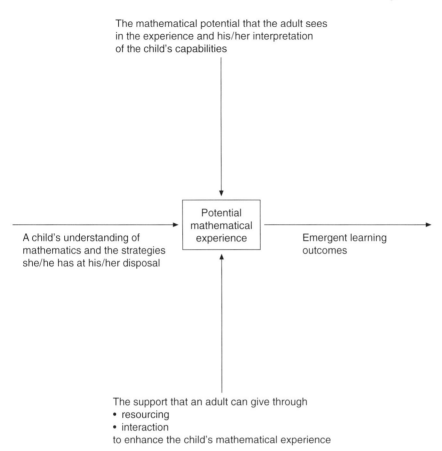

The mathematical potential that the adult sees
in the experience and his/her interpretation
of the child's capabilities

Potential
mathematical
experience

A child's understanding of
mathematics and the strategies
she/he has at his/her disposal

Emergent learning
outcomes

The support that an adult can give through
• resourcing
• interaction
to enhance the child's mathematical experience

Figure 7.2   A model for guiding the mathematical participation of children

In order to help children develop as mathematical thinkers, adults need to understand how children are interpreting the mathematical potential in the experience and understand how they can help children see a little more of the mathematics available. As Saxe *et al.* (1987) suggest in the area of numeracy, this is done by helping children see how mathematics can be used in the situation and then by helping them develop the strategies they need to engage with the mathematics.

Figure 7.2 can help us see what is happening when young children encounter mathematical experiences. We can see from Figure 7.2 that adults have to make two analyses if they are to enhance the mathematics in a child's experience. They have to recognize the mathematical potential themselves and they have to interpret how the child is also likely to experience it. They then use these analyses to make judgements about how they might help the child see a little more of the mathematics and use or develop the wherewithal to deal mathematically with what they see. Having made these judgements adults then make pedagogical decisions about how to help children to see and respond. Adults help by providing particular resources and interacting with children in specific ways. The learning outcomes for children that emerge from mathematical experiences will depend, in part at least, on how adults manage the support that they provide so that a child can participate mathematically in an experience that has mathematical potential. We shall turn to these issues in the next chapter.

However, we shall conclude this chapter by emphasizing the need to help children develop positive dispositions towards mathematics and to do that through a wide variety of enjoyable experiences. De Corte *et al.* (1996: 508), in their comprehensive review of mathematics teaching and learning, talk of developing feelings, sensitivity and inclinations to engage with mathematical opportunities, and of the need for learners to experience mathematics in range of activities: 'the disposition cannot be directly taught but has to develop over an extended period of time; this implies that the organisation of teaching cannot be restricted to a set of discrete goals'.

The comment refers to the learning of mathematics throughout life but is particularly true, we suggest, when thinking about very young children. For early mathematics the lessons from research in mathematics education are that:

- mathematical understanding develops slowly;
- new understandings build on earlier ones so stages cannot be jumped;
- children need a wide range of mathematical experiences;
- mathematical experiences need to be meaningfully embedded in enjoyable activities;
- a disposition to engage with mathematics is crucial;
- adults can help through careful monitoring and by providing conversational support.

The message for educare professionals is, therefore, that children cannot be rushed into performing mathematically. We need to pay attention to how children are making sense of the mathematics around them and encourage them to enjoy thinking mathematically.

 ## Suggested reading

Thompson, I. (ed.) (1997) *Teaching and Learning Early Number* (Buckingham: Open University Press) is an excellent collection of papers on current research on young children and number.

The classic collection of papers on children's thinking and mathematics remains Ginsburg, H. (ed.) (1983) *The Development of Mathematical Thinking* (New York: Academic Press).

A wide-ranging and highly informative review of current research on teaching and learning in mathematics is De Corte, E., Greer, B. and Verschaffel, L. (1996) 'Mathematics teaching and learning', in D. Berliner and R. Calfee (eds) *Handbook of Educational Psychology* (New York: Macmillan).

If you are interested in the ideas on culture and becoming a mathematical thinker we have been discussing you may like to explore these issues more generally through research on mathematics teaching in schools. Seeger, F., Voigt, J. and Waschescio, U. (eds) (1998) *The Culture of the Mathematics Classroom* (Cambridge: Cambridge University Press) is an interesting collection of papers on sociocultural approaches to the learning of mathematics. In the collection a paper by Paul Cobb and Erna Yackel entitled 'A constructivist perspective on the culture of the mathematics classroom' draws on research on 7- and 8-year-olds to tease out the differences between a constructivist view of learning mathematics, which focuses what children learn and how they learn (see the discussion of Piaget in Chapter 4 of this book), and the sociocultural view which focuses on the conditions for the possibilities of learning (see discussion of this topic in Chapter 4 and in this chapter). Cobb and Yackel usefully suggest that both approaches make important contributions to children's mathematical development.

8 How adults support children's mathematical thinking

Guided participation

We have been arguing that young children learn to think mathematically by learning to participate in increasingly knowledgeable ways in the mathematical experiences around them (Saxe *et al.* 1987; Rogoff 1990, 1991). This participation involves them in recognizing the mathematics in an experience and in drawing on the mathematical understandings that they have in order to respond to what they see. For example, when Connor measured his boat in the construction corner he did not hold the tape measure tightly to the end of the boat and did not read the tape measure as 'so many' centimetres. He was beginning to participate mathematically in a construction experience and recognized some aspects of measuring but did not have the mathematical understandings that would allow him to respond in a way that would satisfy, for example, a more expert 10-year-old.

Once one thinks of learning as increasingly knowledgeable responses to the world, the role of adults becomes one of guiding the participation so that a more knowledgeable understanding of the world is constructed by children. It is tempting to think of a curriculum as something we simply pass on to children. But all that we have said about the difficulty of learning number tells us that we need to listen carefully to how young learners are making sense as we assist them to see more and learn how to respond to what they see.

We can best listen and assist in activities that we can share with children. Munn and Schaffer found that good quality interactions in which nursery professionals seemed to be supporting the learning of 2- to 3-year-olds in literacy and numeracy were far more likely to occur where adults worked with smaller groups of children and used a key worker system (Munn and Schaffer 1993). However, they also noted that interactions based on numeracy were generally infrequent. Most of the numeracy activities they observed occurred as parts of stories or songs and were not found in other shared activities. It seemed as if the adults were not aware of the mathematical potential in, for example, shared games or meal times. Kleinburg and Menmuir (1995) used a wider definition of mathematical activity than Munn and Schaffer and found more widespread evidence of mathematical activities. However, they noted that staff were uncertain about what to categorize as a mathematical event and felt that they needed to improve their own mathematical knowledge.

As we have suggested in Figure 7.2 (see page 125), guiding the increasingly knowledgeable participation of children as mathematical thinkers in pre-school provision seems to require three types of knowledge from early years professionals:

- knowledge of what specific children already understand;
- knowledge of the mathematics that is available in the experiences provided;
- knowledge of how to pace their support for children's learning.

We shall look at each of these in turn.

Assessing children's mathematical understanding

Our research partners rapidly concluded that their curriculum development work had to be based on very detailed observations of children as learners. Observational assessment was important for evaluating the experiences they were designing and also for sharing their information on the children as learners with everyone with whom the child would be interacting (see Chapter 3 for further discussion of observations).

Most of the settings kept records of the planned activities that each child experienced. All of them made observational records of children and used them as a basis for their planning for each child. They kept these up to date in a variety of ways. A number of settings used 'post-its' or 'peel off' labels to make immediate notes about what children were understanding in a joint activity and transferred these to the records that were discussed regularly. Others stuck activity record sheets to the walls in areas of the nurseries and used them to make notes on the children, which were immediately available to other adults using the area. Another nursery listed the understandings they wanted to see in action and colleagues carried a child's list while working with him or her and marked off the behaviours with a highlighter pen as they appeared.

Alison and Melissa used the observation schedules we had developed as part of the research and allocated staff to do regular detailed observations of specific children which were then shared. We know, for example, how Connor tackled measurement because we have Polaroid photographs of him measuring and Alison's notes on the activity made under the following headings:

- Who was involved?
- Why you were observing.
- The general intended purpose of the activity, major resources etc.
- The learning opportunities for these children in the activity.
- What happened.
- What the children seemed to learn (with evidence).
- What the adults learnt.

These headings picked up themes that we have been outlining in this chapter such as 'what these children can get out of this activity' and 'what the children can do and understand'. The headings remind the observer to find a focus – that is, 'which children' and 'what aspect of their learning'. They are also open-ended enough to allow the observer to note unexpected events. We can see the flexibility of the schedule in the following example. Toni (the assistant manager of the centre) is observing Owen who is 36 months.

Who was involved?
Owen aged 3 and Toni, in the construction area, 10.30, 15.5.1998.

Why were you observing?
To assess whether Owen knew the names of shapes (especially rectangle). The staff in blue/green room noted that Owen does not use the construction area. He is quite new to the nursery and still finding his feet.

The general intended purpose of the activity
Assess and develop Owen's understanding of shapes (rectangles).

The learning opportunities for these children in the activity
I'm still uncertain what Owen knows. He has still to become familiar with the construction area. Owen will be able to handle and use shapes while I help with names.

What happened
In five minutes during free choice. The full range of equipment was available. Owen was not particularly interested in the construction area before the session. He did not know what a rectangle was. He wanted to go out and play and was embarrassed at being the focus

of my attention. He didn't seem to care whether he knew a rectangle or not.

What the children seemed to learn
Owen was not very interested.

What the adults learnt
It was not very successful and it felt odd and artificial. I had tried to coax Owen into an area he wasn't interested in, at a time when he wanted to play outside, to talk about shapes which he was also not interested in. He is still new to the nursery. I needed to go at his pace so I could have used the words for shapes during our conversations outside. Re: the construction area, I could encourage him to build with the crates and boxes outside.

(Later Toni added the following reflection drawn from Wood 1988 to her notes. While children over 5 are 'recruited' to the curriculum you need to 'capture' the imagination and interest of younger children.)

Toni's observation of Owen had been informed by earlier observations made by colleagues and was shared at the next meeting with colleagues so that others were able to follow her advice on interacting with him.

Knowing the mathematics available in an experience

This is a crucial factor in the guidance that adults can give and explains why so much emphasis is currently being placed on teachers' 'subject knowledge' in primary schools (see Edwards and Knight 1994 for a discussion of the impact of subject teaching on early years practice). However, we prefer to talk of 'curriculum knowledge' as that helpfully places some boundaries on what early years workers need to know. We define curriculum knowledge in pre-school settings as the knowledge opportunities that early years workers offer young learners.

The warp and the weft of curriculum knowledge are (i) *content* – what it is we want children to understand and (ii) *orientation* – how we would like children to tackle the experiences we offer them. These two strands are fundamental to every curriculum area. In the area of mathematics the content would include, for example, using cardinal numbers or distinguishing between a square and a rectangle. Orientation would include a disposition to engage with the experience (see Chapter 4), but most specifically a disposition to engage mathematically. That is, to show a way of thinking that will stand the child in good stead when working mathematically when older. Depending on the age of the child, mathematical orientation may include finding a way of remembering where she or he started to count, organizing objects into sets, aiming at accuracy when

weighing or measuring, learning to record his or her mathematical thinking, recognizing patterns and so on. In summary, to see the mathematics
in situations children need to acquire mathematical habits of mind.

The warp and the weft of curricula become clear as early years professionals plan for children's learning. Team planning helps everyone understand the potential for learning lying in each activity and prepares them
for supporting children's developing understandings and orientations.

Melissa and her colleagues in their High Scope nursery school were using the research partnership to both enrich the mathematics experiences
provided for their 3- and 4-year-olds and to update their own understandings of the curricular potential in the activities available. Melissa used the
observation headings we discussed in the previous section as the basis of
her planning meetings. Colleagues identified the children who were to have
the experience under discussion and the meetings focused on the reasons
for observation, the purposes of the activity and the learning potential in
the activity for the children being targeted, so that everyone could understand what mathematics was available in the activity. The remaining sections
of the schedule were completed during an observation of target children.

One of the most important features in Melissa's project turned out to
be the impact that team planning had on her colleagues. The impact was
seen in two ways: (i) they had a clear focus for their own observations and
actions to support children as learners; (ii) their observations and discussions of them made Melissa's colleagues more aware of what the children
understood and how they were able to respond when tasks were made
slightly more demanding. In summary, armed with greater understanding of the learning potential in activities they were more confident and
flexible in the challenge and support they provided for the children.

In Melissa's nursery we observed a group of staff who were becoming
increasingly confident in their own capacity to see the mathematics in
children's experiences. Research on infant school teachers and the way
that they think about mathematics (Aubrey 1997b) shows very clearly
how teachers' own understandings and beliefs about the subject shape the
way that they organize mathematics in their classrooms and interact with
children in mathematics sessions. In our partnership some people were
alert to the mathematics in almost every aspect of nursery life to the
extent that a striped T-shirt could not be worn without some impromptu
pattern game. Others found that they had to plan in fine detail and
specify language to be used in order to ensure that mathematics occurred.

However, we would argue that the knowledge base of a fully-fledged
educare profession should have an awareness of children's early mathematical understanding as a major strand so that pre-school professionals
don't fall into the trap identified by De Corte *et al.* (1996: 508) and limit
their teaching to 'a discrete set of goals'. Instead, guided participation
means that adults need to be able to work interactively with children so

that they follow a child in order to lead. Following in order to lead means that early years workers need to recognize the variety of learning opportunities available in specific experiences and be alert to how they can connect the learning child to the curricular opportunities available. But as Toni found, capturing young children's attention and connecting them to the opportunities for learning isn't easy!

Pacing support for children as learners

In their study of children from 2 years and 6 months to 5, and their mothers, Saxe *et al.* (1987) found that children were learning through being given opportunities to build on number strategies they already possessed in order to deal with new mathematical demands in activities. The mothers achieved this by gradually making the level of joint activities slightly more demanding. They did this by changing the activity, for example, by first playing a card game with low numbers and then including higher number cards in the game, or by gradually withdrawing the help they gave in reading the numbers on the cards so that the child had to count the hearts or spades in order to 'read' the number.

One way of interpreting the mother's role is to see it simply as modelling how to play the game and then raising the task demand just enough for her child to be able to use the skills she or he already had as he or she acquired new ones. But this is to underplay the joint nature of the activity, the frequency with which it was played and its history in the relationship of the mother and her child, its playfulness and the emotional security provided by the mother-child relationship. Guided participation is clearly valuable but needs careful organization if it is to become a central part of the repertoire of early years workers.

Joint activities were central to Melissa's practice. Records of her planning meetings show how she emphasized being a role model and then an observer or listener. The notes from one meeting gives some flavour.

> The role of the adults in the construction area (children are to be encouraged to use play people so that they need to use the language of position – in, on, outside etc.)
> 1 Role model: while working with children, adults talk about where the child is putting the play people, vehicles and furniture to stimulate discussion and child talk.
> 2 Observer/listener: the adult observes and listens to the child's actions and interactions. This will provide knowledge of the child's skills and evidence on which to base further interactions.

Of course one cannot be a role model without being in the action. In the next extract we see Sarah after the planning meeting noted above with two children aged 4 years and 4 months and 4 years and 2 months. They are in the construction area, have just built a tower block of flats like those outside the nursery and are placing play people on the tower.

Sarah: I really think it's like the flats. Is that right?
Child 1: Mmm, yeh, Look at 'em on top.
Child 2: Look, four – one, two, three, four.
Sarah: Oh yes. There are four people on top of the flats and they are all looking that way (*points*). Who's at the bottom?
Child 1: It's a boy. He's going out to play. Look she lives upstairs (*pointing*).
Sarah: Oh I can see. She lives above the boy. What's she called?
Child 2: Sarah (*giggles*).
Sarah: Same name as me then. That's good.
Child 1: That one's me (*pointing*).
Sarah: Are you going to the bottom, the top, or are you in the middle?
Child 2: She's not. She's not.
Sarah: No, not at the top, not at the bottom, not in the middle! But where? Where do you call that?
Child 2: Nearly. Nearly the top – nearly the middle. If she is up, then top (*moves figure up the tower*).

In this extract we see that Sarah was involved in a playful activity with the two children; was looking at the activity, in part, through their eyes; was able conversationally to extend the activity; and, through the conversation and playfulness (for example, 'where do you call that?'), was able to provide spaces for the children to contribute and construct understandings. Sarah's primary purpose was not to test the children, but a great deal of useful information about the children is revealed and Sarah is able to build on it as the conversation continues. In summary, she was helping the children to see more of the mathematics available in the activity and to find the wherewithal to deal with it. She was assisted in both aims by being part of the action.

In Chapter 4 we talked about how adults can scaffold the learning of young children. Here we see Sarah scaffolding – that is, providing support and challenge, for the thinking of two 4-year-olds. We emphasized that scaffolding is not simply a question of explaining and then leaving the child to work with the activity. Rather, scaffolding is more like an interactive dance requiring that the adult assist, stand back and assist again if the child needs it. Pacing the support requires being attuned to the child's way of seeing and responding but also being aware of the overall structure of the dance and the possibilities within it. Pacing also, therefore, needs to take into account children's developmental needs.

In Chapter 4 we discussed how adults' scaffolding aims at bringing children to understand the world more effectively and that it has slightly different purposes as children develop. In that chapter we talked of the initial intersubjective relationship that carers have with babies, how carers help children to explore the world beyond that relationship and finally how, through sound relationships with the adults in their worlds, children are helped to act increasingly independently.

Our research partners found that the most important feature of their work over the two years of the project was not the activities that they designed to help children to use number. Rather it was the quality of the staff interactions around the activities. In our final workshop, therefore, we identified ways in which adults can support children as learners who are developing a disposition to engage with mathematics. These are shown in Table 8.1.

Table 8.1   Principles of practice in supporting pleasurable participation in mathematics

What we are looking for in children	What adults can do
	0–12 months
• Pleasurable responses	• Give warmth and pleasure
• Alertness	• Model
• Exploration	• Play sorting games
	• Find patterns in songs
Later	• Find consistent patterns in games
• Building	• Find consistent behaviour in routines
• Sorting	• Play body-parts games
• Posting	• Do counting with finger food
• Putting things in	• Sing number rhymes (e.g. 1, 2, 3, 4, 5 etc.)
	• Share (e.g. at meal time)
	12–18 months
• Sorting by size and building	• As above
• Posting	• Encourage modelling by older children and adults
• Exploration	• Water play
• Joining-in singing	• Make the most of domestic situations (e.g. mealtimes)
• One-to-one	• Dressmaking
• Matching with guidance	• Dressing
• Enjoy water and sand	• Gardening
	• Cooking
	• Sing number songs children can join in
	• Allowing children to be part of adults' experience
	• Allow children to anticipate patterns in fabric, knitting etc.

Table 8.1   (cont'd)

What we are looking for in children	What adults can do
18–24 months	
• Full and empty	• As above, slightly more focused
• Know number rhymes	• Make more demands on child (e.g. get me two pots)
• Matching	• Give instructions (e.g. walking in twos)
At 24 months	• Sing more rhymes
• Have partners (e.g. walking in twos)	• Counting stairs/steps
• Imitate language patterns	• Allow help with setting table and putting away
• Be responsive	• Sorting
• Take initiative with number	• In the park (e.g. see-saw, up-down)
	• Thinking aloud when using numbers
24–36 months	
• Purposeful/systematic behaviour	• As above, slightly more focused
• Concrete use of, e.g., 2	• Children asked to set table
• Start of understanding of quality	• Help children with matching games
• Using mathematical language	• Ask children questions which require numerical answers
	• Help children make collections (e.g. buttons, shells)
36–60 months	
• Closer relationship between language and accepted meaning	• As above, more focused, higher expectations of children's language use
• Appear to be getting more from working with other children	• Play guessing games using number
• Ordinal/cardinal differences	• Help with sorting collections into sets
• Start sensible estimates	• Model measuring, recording etc.
• Start symbolic recording (iconic)	• Provide materials to extend children's mathematical thinking
• Number as *fun*	• Play number games

◯ Providing mathematical experiences

In Chapter 4 we explained that learning involves becoming competent at using the tools of a culture. These tools include the language of mathematics (how we count or name shapes and the language formats of mathematics such as 'one more'), ways of working in mathematics (how we record our mathematical thinking or emphasize accuracy) and material artefacts (a tape measure or a weighing scale). In the present chapter we have discussed how children experience mathematical activities at their level of competence and have shown that part of the role of adults is to help them extend that competence by seeing other opportunities in the activity. Therefore, although we shall now discuss a number of the curricular opportunities that were developed in the partnership we stress that children will work with them in a variety of ways and adult support should tailor the activity to the strengths and needs of children.

We know that children enter formal schooling at 5 with a considerable amount of mathematical cultural capital. That is, they have had experience of, for example, number, shape and capacity, and use what they have gained from these experiences as the foundation of their mathematical learning in school. However, children's capital can vary quite considerably due to differences between their environments in the first five years of life. One of the purposes of pre-school educational provision is to ensure that as many children as possible experience the activities that provide valuable capital. We have been arguing that pre-school provision is therefore not meant to be a watered down version of school but an enriched version of some aspects of home.

Our research partners operated with that principle very much in mind as they developed materials and activities in their settings. A strong feature in almost all the activities developed was their 'everydayness'. These were activities that would be found in the homes of most advantaged children made slightly more focused by the careful resourcing and sensitive interventions of staff. We shall look at some of the activities and research projects by grouping them rather arbitrarily under three headings: birth to 18 months, 18 months to 3 years and 3 to 5 years. These phases broadly represent the phases from intersubjectivity to independence that we outlined in Chapter 4.

Birth to 18 months

A songbook. Millie and Amy's nursery is situated on an estate near a city centre and is used by parents who work in the city as well as by local residents. Babies enter the nursery when they are 3 months old and stay in the baby room until they are toddlers and need more space. Millie and Amy were keen to provide continuity of care with the children's homes and produced the songbook we mentioned in Chapter 4 when we discussed intersubjectivity. The songs in the book were selected to augment the children's mathematical capital. There were number rhymes (e.g. 'Round and round the garden'); songs with repetitive patterns (e.g. 'Pat-a-cake' and 'Peep-o'); and songs associated with bathtime or dressing and parts of the body (e.g. 'Two little eyes').

The songbooks were welcomed both by the young mothers who lived locally and the busy working mothers, and alerted them to how they could playfully help their children to become receptive to number.

Millie and Amy involved all the staff in compiling the book and simultaneously alerted them to the value of number songs as a fun way of bringing number into the experiences they offered children throughout the nursery.

Building on experiences from several cultures. Reza, a multicultural services officer, and June, the head of an inner-city nursery, decided to explore the capital that the children were bringing to the nursery from their homes. Children in the nursery between them spoke 20 languages. June and Reza invited parents to the nursery to discuss their project and how they were keen to ensure that the nursery was aware of what the children were learning at home.

June visited five of the families regularly and listened as the parents chatted about their children's growing interest in the mathematics around them. An important learning point for June and her colleagues was that the parents used songs in very different ways from that suggested by the nursery. Songs were sung by the whole family in Arabic-speaking homes and were sung for different purposes – for example, ballads for storying, lullabies at bedtime and strongly rhythmical songs for dancing.

Importantly, the learning was two-way. The parents became more aware of how they could help their children see the numbers around them as they grew older and the nursery staff learnt that they needed to work with the cultural opportunities available in the children's homes and develop materials that fitted into the rhythms of the children's cultural lives at home. Parents were invited to contribute their own family favourites to a multilingual nursery songbook.

18 months to 3 years

A musical curriculum. Frances runs a workplace nursery which takes children from 2 years of age. Songs and singing lie at the centre of Frances' practice. As part of their project Frances and her colleagues brainstormed the *skills, concepts* and *attitudes* involved in making music. They came up with the following list:

listening	concentrating	discriminating
organizing	cooperation	fine and gross motor control
consideration	discussion	memory
self-discipline	problem solving	sharing
decision making	independence	imagination
critical awareness	mutual respect	tolerance
perseverance	sense of achievement	caring
enthusiasm	positive self-image	confidence
enjoyment	curiosity	empathy

As the project progressed they saw that they could combine these important curricular aims with focuses which gave children mathematical experiences. These included clapping to musical patterns, sitting in large and small circles, ordering children by size in action songs, number rhymes involving counting, some simple rhymes involving making sets of children or objects and using cardinal numbers, adding or removing one child or object at a time, and action games requiring children to work in pairs and match actions. Songs such as 'Peter hammers with one hammer' played an important part in the children's introduction to number as fun.

In all of these examples the familiar patterns of the songs acted as a form of scaffolding in which younger children could first see adults and other children model behaviour, and then imitate the actions and appropriate the language before being able to fully understand the rules and meanings of the activity.

Making the most of everyday mathematics. Josie runs a large nursery school on the outskirts of a city. Everywhere you turn in her nursery you see evidence of children's mathematical thinking. Colour mixing activities lead to pattern making, the progress of the newly-hatched ducklings is monitored using counting, short sorting activities or number games greet parents and children as they arrive at the school, one-to-one matching occurs in the home, construction, design and technology areas and recording are built into role play in the shop or cafe. Josie and her colleagues clearly have mathematical thinking as a priority. Josie was keen that parents shared her enthusiasm for mathematics, not only to help the children already attending the school, but also to prepare younger family members. Preparation is important, as local school placement policies mean that children stay in Josie's nursery for no longer than a year. Children therefore need to be ready to make the most of the opportunities available to them when they arrive.

Josie was already familiar with the excellent work on parental involvement in primary school mathematics carried out by the IMPACT project team (Merttens and Vass 1990, 1993) and wanted to build on their ideas as she strengthened relationships with her parents. She started by inviting parents of children entering the nursery to a 30-minute meeting where she talked about the mathematical learning children are experiencing at home. Parents' interest in the topic led to a series of evening meetings and a partnership with the local adult education services which set up afternoon classes for interested parents on 'parents as partners' in their children's education. The major themes in Josie's work with parents were acknowledging what parents had to offer and encouraging them to see just how mathematically rich the home environment is.

After exploring the learning opportunities at home with their own young children the parents made booklets for other parents on, for example, maths in the bathroom, maths at mealtimes, maths in the kitchen. Parents also took pictures of their children sorting shoes into pairs, making sets of lipsticks and nail varnishes, counting steps in the garden and so on. The photographs were then shared and discussed at parents' meetings. We met the parents who were involved several times during the project and found their enthusiasm and inventiveness inexhaustible and their appreciation of what the nursery school was doing with their children while they were there impressive.

Working with childminders to make the most of everyday mathematics. Gill was the only childminder involved in the project. She set up regular meetings of a small group of childminders and discussed the ideas that were being discussed in the project. Gill reported that they focused on 'spontaneously available learning opportunities' which occurred from 'children's everyday activities or interests'. At meetings the group brainstormed ideas about everyday mathematical experiences such as seeing shapes, playing with patterns and using number.

They all kept a daily numeracy diary in which they logged activities which could offer the children opportunities for mathematical thinking. At their meetings they discussed what they did to enhance children's mathematical experiences. Areas of activity focused on patterns and shape; comparisons and problem solving in, for example, cooking or planning a day out; the language of position, size and shape in, for example, games and putting things away; and numbers in the world about them, in counting games and in dressing.

They felt strongly that they needed to be alert to the opportunities in activities and enjoyed being able to evaluate their own roles in encouraging children to participate in those opportunities. In summary, they had the advantage of strong and consistent links with the children they saw (usually daily) and were also able to think as practitioners about how to assist children as learners.

3 to 5 years

We have already discussed at some length the mathematical experiences provided by Alison and Melissa in their construction areas. In our discussions we emphasized three features:

- careful resourcing – for example, the tape measure and recording opportunities in Alison's project and the play people in Melissa's;
- the open-ended nature of the opportunities they provided so that children could work with the skills they had;
- the playfully interactive role of the adults so that they could model language and responses and raise the demands of the activity when necessary.

Other examples from our partnership included Bernie's project with Claire, the teacher in an inner-city multicultural nursery and Jade's work in the outer-city nursery where she was the teacher attached to the nursery.

Number as an international language. Bernie, like Reza, worked for the city's multicultural services and was attached to Claire's centre. Together, they decided to focus on specific cardinal numbers and give children the opportunity to work with a variety of sets of one cardinal number over the period of one month at a time. They decided to focus on the target numeral to enhance children's number literacy, regardless of their ability to speak English. The one-month focus on each number allowed parental involvement by providing sets of small objects (e.g. coins or buttons) and number songs from home, and gave time to work with the numbers in the children's mother tongues as well as in English. The tight focus and long timescale also helped to secure the attention of volunteer workers to the nursery's curricular aims.

Activities in the 'fives' month included: number rhymes such as 'Five in a bed' and 'Five little speckled frogs' with song cards to take home; the collection of sets of fives for display; organizing children into groups of five for activities; sorting objects into sets of five; finding ways of recording five; writing fives in the sand; setting the table in the home area for five people; planting five seedlings in pots; feely bags with five objects in them; clapping rhythms with five beats; building the longest road with five blocks, and so on.

Everyday mathematics in the neighbourhood. Jade's project was beset by problems including vandalism and flooding. However, she did not give up. Parental involvement was a priority for the centre in which she was the nursery teacher. The centre is situated on an estate on the edge of a large city, not far from a large out-of-town shopping mall. The parents are mainly young single parents who have strong negative feelings about school which are based on their own quite recent experiences as pupils. There is also a small Urdu-speaking population. Parents see the centre primarily as place for care and not for education.

To encourage parental confidence in the centre's abilities to help their children value learning, Jade planned a mathematics trail in the shopping mall. She used the trail to highlight the everyday mathematical experiences that children and parents might share on a visit to the shops. She and her colleagues produced two information packs. One focused on shapes and used photographs that staff had taken at the mall. The photographs included shop signs, patterns of windows, floor tiles, fabric patterns and a map of the mall. The second pack consisted of a set of questions or prompts to guide parents' conversations as they walked around the mall with their children. The questions or prompts included: 'Look at the floors, walls and ceiling. What patterns can you see?';

'Can you see any triangles?'; 'What numbers can you see in the shop windows?'

The first pack was discussed with parents at a meeting before the visit to the mall. Parents were then given the second pack as they set off for the mall with their children and some of the centre staff. While they were on the trail, staff modelled how to help the children see the everyday mathematics around them and encouraged the parents to do the same. Parents took photographs of their children having fun with mathematics.

The photographs were enjoyed at a follow-up meeting with the parents arranged by Jade. At the meeting there were more conversations about the mathematics that were experienced and parents' confidence in their abilities to help their children use aspects of mathematics was again encouraged. A book about shape and number based on the visit was produced in both English and Urdu and was made available to all parents.

Summary

Our research partnership consisted of a network of people who aimed at trialing a small number of activities in either numeracy or literacy for children from birth to 5. Consequently we are not offering an exhaustive list of tips for early years workers. Even if that had been our intention we would have been deterred by the feedback we received from our research partners. The messages from the pre-school settings was that far more important than the activities provided is the quality of the interaction that occurs around them. We therefore are not offering the activities mentioned in this chapter as blueprints for a pre-school mathematics curriculum. Instead we are suggesting a careful process of trial and evaluation which emphasizes attention to both what the children and the staff are learning as they engage with the mathematical opportunities available in pre-school settings and at home.

Suggested reading

A detailed and useful introduction to the theory and the practice of providing mathematical experiences in pre-schools is Montague-Smith, A. (1997) *Mathematics in Nursery Education* (London: David Fulton).

A well-informed yet highly practical response to the requirements of *Desirable Outcomes for Learning* is *Learning Mathematics in the Early Years: Desirable Approaches,* compiled by the Early Childhood Mathematics Group and published in 1997 by BEAM with the support of Islington Council at BEAM, Barnsbury Complex, Offord Road, London, N1 1QH.

If you are interested in teachers' knowledge and its impact on how mathematics is taught in the early years, Carol Aubrey's account of the thinking and practice of infant teachers is a comprehensive study of this topic: Aubrey, C. (1997a) *Mathematics Teaching in the Early Years* (London: Falmer).

9 Creating contexts for professional development in educare

○ Times of change

As we outlined in Chapter 1 the project took place during a time of rapid change affecting early childhood services in the UK. During the 18-month period of the project we saw a change in government, the withdrawal of the nursery voucher scheme and government consultation papers on education, special educational needs and the family. Inspection systems looking at the educational aspects of early childhood provision became established. Centres of excellence in early childhood were selected for additional government funding (including two in our partner local authorities). Local authority development plans for early childhood were put in place. Early years fora were set up locally. Early childhood degrees proliferated and even the most traditional of universities welcomed practitioners as part-time students. It became increasingly clear that, at last, early childhood provision was to get the attention it deserved. As a result of that attention, the changes during the 18 months of the project were to be only the beginning of an exciting period for the development of provision.

If we return to Bronfenbrenner's (1979) ecological analysis of the contexts of children's learning discussed in Chapter 1 and consider the changes in priorities, policies and practices relating to the learning of children from birth to 5 in pre-school settings, we can see a system experiencing some quite profound shifts. Bronfenbrenner's analysis reminds us that these changes are interconnected and reverberate long after initial policy decisions are made. Our project aimed at working with these shifts in order to enable practitioners to develop a form of professional educare practice that would allow them to meet foreseeable new demands and to deal with those that were yet to come. Our aims could be summarized as helping to create learning professionals who could deal with changes in informed and systematic ways.

In this chapter we look at professional learning for educare in a changing system: the learning of individuals; the contexts in which their learning takes place; and what this learning means for practice, training and management. We use the term 'learning' rather than 'coping' not simply because we want to avoid the rather negative tone of coping, but also because we believe that dealing with change is a matter of simply learning something new and taking a positive approach to that learning. We are therefore optimistic that an area of provision that has expertise in helping children learn will also be good at helping adults learn.

All that we have discussed in the last five chapters tells us that sound quality interactions with adults are central to the development of children's dispositions to learn. It is a truism, but nonetheless a powerful one, that children learn to love learning through being with adults who also love to learn, and are themselves in contexts that encourage their learning. This truism, therefore, means that children deserve to be supported by adults who are driven by their own intellectual curiosity to understand their practice better. Children's learning, we would argue, is supported by a system that has the learning of both children and adults as a priority.

 ## Educare as a community of practice?

The development of the profession and knowledge base of educare that we monitored during the project was particularly challenging for pre-school services because of the quite radical changes in practice necessary in pockets of provision. In Chapter 3 we described our aims as helping to create an informed *community of practice* of educare. The goal of an informed community of practice is important for the development of educare as a new form of professional practice. The idea of a community of practice comes from the work of psychologists and anthropologists who have researched how knowledge is used and shared in communities of practitioners (Lave and Wenger 1991; Chaiklin and Lave 1993).

Communities of practice are seen as knowledge communities that create and use their understandings of practice in quite specific ways. For example, the knowledge community of children's nursing is very different from the knowledge community of children's welfare work and both are different from early years teaching. The knowledge found in communities of practice is often tacit and therefore not open to public scrutiny. Instead, knowledge of practice is understood, used and developed in the context of the practice. New members of a knowledge community are brought into established practices by learning to participate in the practices. For example, student nursery nurses become members of the community of practice of nursery nursing, first through observation, then through some marginal activities and finally by working alongside experts to use the knowledge of the practices they have been gaining through observation and simple tasks.

Learning through participation in traditional practices is a very power-ful model of learning and one that has dominated in the training of nursery nurses and, more recently, teachers. It makes a great deal of sense when we are helping people learn to work as professionals in complex settings such as pre-school. However, the idea of a community of practice as a place for passing on traditions also reveals some of the problems facing early years providers. If educare is to have any currency it needs to have coherence, have a knowledge base that can be scrutin-ized, and draw on only the best of recent traditions to meet new chal-lenges. Above all, educare as a form of professional practice has to be forward looking and not simply rely on the passing on of existing ideas of what good practice is.

Therefore, if understandings of practice come through practice itself, forward-looking change has to start simultaneously with changes in practice as well as changes in ways of thinking about practice. The challenge, as we outlined it in Chapter 3, is therefore to create a new community of practice while supporting those who are learning as they develop new practices.

 ## Supporting the learning of practitioners

In Chapter 4 we outlined features of learning in early childhood. A number of these features also apply to how nursery workers learn and how they can be supported. In our project the learning goals for practi-tioners, like those for the children, focused on the *who* as much as on the *what* of learning and particularly on helping participants develop a capacity to interpret and respond to the learning opportunities available for children. The goals included:

- developing the capacity to see the educational potential in experiences shared with children;
- developing the capacity to respond to the demands they have identified as they work with children;
- developing dispositions for enquiry and learning;

- developing ways of seeing and being which draw on the knowledge base of educare.

Like children, adults learn best in safe and well-supported contexts where they are able to learn through a form of *guided participation*. Guided participation is important because we are suggesting that learning the practice of educare is a question of learning to interpret familiar events in fresh ways and developing a repertoire of responses to new interpretations. Fresh interpretations and responses usually need to be modelled or guided and can seem quite risky. Interpretations might be wrong and responses may misfire. Practitioners need support if they are to change their practices.

Support for practitioners' learning through guided participation occurred in two ways in the project (see Chapter 3 for an outline of the project as three steps):

1 collaboration between higher education, local authority officers and the key participants in Steps 1 and 2;
2 collaboration within settings on action research in Step 3.

During these *collaborations* practitioners' learning was *scaffolded* by:

- the modelling of strategies with children by more expert practitioners – for example, when Mollie worked with children on mark-making and was observed by a colleague;
- discussions for planning and reviewing;
- joint data collection and analysis;
- shared frameworks for data collection – for example, observation schedules;
- a shared focus on children's learning in numeracy and literacy.

Practitioners' learning through those scaffolding processes became evident in how they used language (for example, the idea of joint involvement episodes became central to several projects); and in how the familiar materials of pre-school provision took on new educational meanings as, for example, the construction area became a site for children's early mark-making in one setting and their mathematical thinking and action in another.

In the structured and non-threatening learning contexts provided by the action research projects practitioners were able, in their discussions, to *appropriate* the frameworks and language of early learning shared in the workshops and readings. Similarly, while they worked with these new ideas with children they were able to identify the educational potential of familiar materials – such as how blocks and play people could be used together to develop children's use of mathematical language in a fantasy play context – and respond knowledgeably.

We were interested to note in our repertory grid analysis discussed in Chapter 3 (see Table 3.4) that participants did not identify a need for new resources as a result of an increased emphasis on curricula. Instead, and our field notes would confirm this, existing materials were being given new (educational) meanings by practitioners. The changes appeared to be in how the adults were interpreting events and responding while working with children. The professional learning that occurred through well-supported participation in new forms of practice seemed considerable. Like the children, the adults learnt through participating in experiences which demanded specific (i.e. in this case educational) ways of thinking and acting. But like children, adults can only change their ways of thinking and acting in contexts that allow these changes to occur. Learning contexts for adults, therefore, need careful management.

 ## Current work on educational settings as learning organizations

Our emphasis on the *who* of learning – that is, the development of informed professional identities capable of making the responsive decisions that are so much part of supporting young children as learners, took us to an examination of the strategies that the most successful managers used to support the professional development of colleagues.

There is a vast literature on school development, some of which focuses on educational change through the professional development of teachers. So much valuable work has been undertaken in this field that it would be somewhat narrow-minded of educare professionals if they were to ignore it. The work we shall discuss has been influenced by methods of person-centred organizational development found in commercial and industrial organizations, and emphasizes professional learning as the key to informed responses to external changes. Michael Fullan's (1991) comprehensive review of research on educational change in the contexts of educational reform in North America provides many useful pointers for institution-based professional learning for educare professionals. Above all he reminds us that changing hearts and minds is also a question of changing cultures, that change is usually complex and rarely straightforward, that it needs to be managed by supporting the learning of colleagues as they develop new ideas in practice, that it takes time and is far more than a question of simply setting targets.

We outlined our project as a change process in Chapter 3. The goal of our project was not simply to ensure that our practitioner partners could work towards *Desirable Outcomes for Learning* (DfEE/SCAA 1996a) (we could not even assume that the document would still be in use at the end of the project, given recent policy swings) but to ensure that they were able to develop strategies for dealing with changing contexts in informed ways. We intended that the project would give key participants experiences of frameworks for evidence-based practice which would help them develop their colleagues as educarers. Our focus was therefore as much on the adults as learners as on the pupils. Because of the focus, our concern was the development of the pre-school settings as learning communities.

Louis *et al.* (1996), in a detailed study of teachers' professional communities identified five components which they found to be significant in schools as learning communities which in turn supported children as learners. These components were:

1 a shared sense of purpose;
2 a collective focus on pupil learning;
3 collaborative activity;
4 deprivatized activity;
5 reflective dialogues.

A shared sense of purpose takes time to achieve and can't be imposed. Quite often a sense of coherent purpose only emerges in the processes of discussion and action as colleagues clarify exactly what they mean by, for example, the community values underpinning the work of a pre-school centre. Fullan (1991, 1993) points out that one sign that change is not really happening is when people demonstrate 'false clarity' – for example, the rhetoric is spoken and accepted but the implications for practice are barely explored. Parental involvement is an area where false clarity is frequently seen. False clarity is evident, for example, when parental involvement is discussed as a 'good thing' without anyone being clear about what they really think parents can do to help their children learn. In our study, as we shall see later in this chapter, our colleagues took the time necessary to move way beyond any sense of false clarity in their work with parents and identified coherent rationales for parental involvement.

A collective focus on pupil learning allows the development of a professional discourse which centres on the professional actions of colleagues as they create contexts and plan and evaluate actions taken to support children's learning. In our study two strong themes in the collective focus on children's learning were (i) detailed and clearly focused observations of how children were making sense of the opportunities available to them and (ii) careful consideration of how adults interacted with children while they engaged with the materials provided.

Collaborative activity is essential for the development of a professional discourse of educare and the professional learning of educarers. We have proposed that learning occurs as people take action and interpret and react to events in increasingly informed ways – i.e. as they become people who see and act differently. Knowledge, we have therefore argued, is constructed in action as well as in discussions of action. Collaborative activity was central to our study, particularly at Step 3 where new understandings were developed in action in pre-school settings. Here our research partners, having undertaken some small-scale work themselves at Step 2, were able to guide the participation of other colleagues in the practices they were developing.

Deprivatized activity links closely to both a collective focus on learning and taking action together. Compared with schools, most pre-school settings are well placed for ensuring that adults' activities are visible. What did have to be worked at was finding space for the open discussion of activities in which new practices were tried out or modelled. Key activities became the focus of frequent staff meetings in which areas for action were identified, strategies selected and the evidence gathered during the activities was discussed. Early childhood services in Reggio Emilia similarly emphasize deprivatized activity in the stress they place on documenting their work to ensure that their practices are visible to colleagues and parents (Edwards *et al.* 1993). These documents not only render expert practice visible but enable colleagues to respond more coherently to children.

Reflective dialogues, in which evidence either about the settings or action taken is discussed, encourage careful observation and analysis and the sharing of insights and information. But above all they ensure that the tacit expertise of professionals is revealed. Reflective dialogues were a feature of all three steps in our project and occurred between higher education and the key settings-based participants at Step 1, between higher education, key participants and their colleagues at Step 2 and mainly between the key participants and their immediate colleagues at Step 3. These conversations were the vehicles for knowledge exchange and joint knowledge construction and were carefully built into project planning in every step.

We did not explore the supervision systems at work in the collaborating settings in this project. However, there is evidence to suggest that supervisory practices which focus on professional issues, attend to the personal development of practitioners, emphasize the learning of individuals and groups and allow roles and practices to develop responsively are found in cultures usually described as developmental or learning (Hawkins and Shohet 1989). We would argue that supervisory systems for educarers in many ways parallel key worker systems for children. Good quality supervision which focuses on how adults are helping children develop as learners and encourages reflective dialogue based on evidence and joint activities may prove to be one important driver of change in educare.

Working for professional development across institutional boundaries

Dahlberg and Åsén (1994) take the idea of visibility and discussion of practices further than the school-based concerns of Louis *et al.* (1996) and the cross-settings focus of our project. Dahlberg and Åsén discuss the public fora or *plazas* that were emerging in Sweden in the early 1990s. These plazas were set up as arenas for locally based public discussion between politicians, teachers, administrators and other early years professionals. Discussions in plazas range over policy and pedagogy and concern themselves with local, regional and national issues. Dahlberg and Åsén argue that plazas should be seen as places for 'a dialogue between independent citizens' (1994: 167) and through the informed discussions that occur, early childhood professional practice will be brought more overtly into the public arena. Their argument is that these plazas can assist in achieving widespread public support for forms of early childhood provision which meet the current and future needs of children. This support, they suggest, will come as a result of engagement in early childhood issues by the citizens of a democratic state with responsibility for the well-being of children.

Swedish plazas appear to be different in intention from the 'early years fora' proposed in the 1997 Green Paper, *Excellence in Schools* (DfEE 1997). The Green Paper indicated that early years fora are more focused on achieving integration of services than the professional emancipation that lies behind the arguments presented by Dahlberg and Åsén. However, as opportunities to openly discuss provision and share insights and intelligence, the fora have the potential to create contexts for professional learning at local levels.

We have so far outlined three levels of change in the development of educare as a profession: (i) individual professional learning; (ii) institutional strategies to support professional learning; and (iii) developments in local contexts that aim to encourage professional learning across institutional boundaries. In addition we have noted that change at each of these levels, in line with Bronfenbrenner's (1979) analysis, is enabled by the current national policy emphasis on educational focuses in early childhood services. As our focus in this chapter is the professional development of educarers we now turn to examine how professional learning in our research project was enhanced through working across professional and locational boundaries and through opening up practice to ideas that refreshed and, at times, transformed it.

Work at the boundaries of institutional settings was an important feature of the project, whether this was with parents, other professional groups, or colleagues in other settings or other local authorities. We would argue that if educare is to develop as an informed profession able to meet the shifts and challenges of, in the UK at least, a political context bent on modernizing (Giddens 1998), informed flexibility and openness to new ways of interpreting and responding in practice is essential. As we explored what was happening when we were open to new ideas and worked across boundaries we found one important common feature.

Every sustained interaction across boundaries which seemed to result in learning involved what Engeström, writing within a sociocultural framework, describes as a 'problem space' 'at which an activity is directed' (Engeström 1993: 67). Joint action around a common set of interests to which different perspectives and strengths could be brought to bear was central to our project. The research project itself seemed to become a safe yet challenging space in which meanings could be shared and developed. For example, the project enabled colleagues to operate across the boundaries of their own professional settings and the histories of their own professional backgrounds and to use common research strategies on a set of common problems associated with children's early learning in literacy and mathematics. Through the project, as we saw in Chapter 3, practitioners were able to develop a growing sense of being members of a knowledge community of educare and confidently make their tacitly held professional knowledge explicit in ways that could be shared with other participants.

At the level of individual settings and their boundaries with their local communities, we found that those projects which involved working with parents passed materials between home and school and used these shared objects as opportunities to jointly build understandings of the children as learners both at home and at nursery. In Engeström's terms these materials became the focal point of activity at the boundaries between home and school. The materials included booklets about the children and what they could do, songs and nursery rhymes written on cards or in booklets, and number sets that children had constructed at home. Importantly, these objects were used both to enable practitioners to learn about the children as learners at home and to help parents to understand how they could support their children as participants in, for example, literacy while at home.

Let us therefore look in a little more detail at how learning relationships were sustained through links between settings, other agencies, the community, adult education, higher education, parents, and other types of pre-school provision.

Working with other agencies

Speech therapy. Ivy's project, discussed in Chapter 6, involved her learning while working alongside speech therapists while Ivy herself guided the learning of the mothers on whom her project was focused. Ivy collaborated with speech therapists in devising a tightly focused learning programme for the mothers which aimed at developing their interaction skills with their children. The project drew on the ideas about child development and the importance of good quality relationships with caregivers we have outlined in Chapter 4, and shared in workshops in Steps 1 and 2 of the project. The speech therapists' specialist expertise, their experience in developing communication skills and their familiarity with the nursery were invaluable in both planning and carrying out the programme.

A local multicultural service. Bernie and Reza work for the multicultural services section of one of the collaborating local authorities. They were also project members who collaborated with teachers in two inner-city nurseries. Bernie's collaboration focused on number use. Working with a group of practitioners in one nursery, he was able to advise practitioners on how to make the most of the cultural strengths that the children, from up to 11 different ethnic backgrounds, brought to the nursery.

For Reza, the project allowed him to explore a long-held professional hunch: that children's musical experiences at home vary across ethnic groups and that this may have an impact on how they are able to engage with learning experiences in number in nurseries. As we outlined in Chapter 8, he collaborated with June, a nursery-based practitioner, and learnt through the interviews undertaken with parents at home about what the parents from a range of ethnic groupings thought about children's early number experiences at home and in the nursery, and how music was used within each home.

An initiative in another city. Jenny's project, discussed in Chapter 6, was part of a wider local authority initiative which aimed at improving literacy. It targeted specific parents of young infants and built on the Bookstart Project in Birmingham (Book Trust 1998). The project had three aims:

1 to encourage parents to share books with their babies;
2 to raise awareness of how literacy develops in very young children;
3 to raise awareness of the parent's role in helping their children to value literacy.

Jenny's evaluations suggest that, although she was working with ideas gathered during an initial visit to the programme in Birmingham from practitioners there, without the locally-based support for developing her thinking about present practice that was provided by our project she was in danger of being isolated. The lesson here seems to be that being open to ideas from elsewhere is essential, but taking these ideas into practice in ways that transform practice is helped by locally-based opportunities for frequent and detailed discussion of practice.

Working with parents

Singing from the same song sheet. We discussed the songbook produced by Millie and Amy in Chapter 4. We drew on it as an example of how a nursery tried to provide babies with some consistency of experience when they were enjoying finger rhymes and songs at home and in the nursery. We particularly noticed the use of line drawings which reminded both parents and practitioners of how a baby was most usefully held for a particular rhyme or action song. We highlighted this in discussions with Millie and Amy and in workshops, in relation to two features. First, how consistent action and language formats help children develop as language users, and second how interactive songs help children to engage in the conversational give and take they need to experience as early communicators.

The songbook became a space for joint action between parents and practitioners when it was being compiled and when it was used. Parents and staff provided songs and when the book was in use they discussed the children's reactions to individual songs. Discussions about the children and songs helped staff to build on children's experiences with their parents. The book also became a space for discussions about informed practice between nursery and university-based practitioners.

Partnership in early literacy. Meg and her staff at her children's centre on a large outer-city council estate had, for a long time, been keen to involve parents in supporting their children as learners. As we outlined in Chapter 6, Meg started with an unstructured book loan scheme for the 3- and 4-year-olds which brought the parents into the centre to choose books with their children. Our advice was that Meg should work with the parents' strengths – i.e. the strong emotional links they have with their children and make sure that anything they asked parents to do was easily managed and was fun. We discussed nursery rhyme cards that we had seen in use in another project and Meg took up the idea.

Meg produced simple cards with rhymes on one side and suggestions on the reverse. These suggestions included actions to accompany the rhyme, help with finding familiar words in the rhyme, help on how to point to print and ideas for using the same sounds to make up your own rhymes. Parents shared their children's enjoyment with staff when they exchanged cards and appeared to have lost their earlier diffidence about how they might support their children as learners. It seemed that the book and card loan scheme with their realistic expectations broke a barrier between home and nursery that had been troubling Meg.

Involving parents and adult learning support services. Josie's project on parental involvement in early mathematical thinking is discussed in Chapter 8. Josie's nursery is situated in an area of private housing on the outskirts of a city. The parents are keen supporters of the nursery and attend in large numbers any workshop or meeting she holds. So keen were the parents during the project that Josie could have found herself becoming an adult educator rather than a pre-school specialist.

The solution was to involve the local authority's adult learning support service. At various stages in the project this service provided regular classes for parents which had the effect of raising parents' own sense of self-efficacy and leading them to either job-seeking or further training. The service also provided workshops in the nursery during the nursery day on early number development at home.

We would suggest that this is an option which is always worth exploring as local targets for women's access to training or the participation of certain ethnic groups in local training opportunities may mean that funding is easily available. Josie certainly valued the support provided. She brought the adult educator quite centrally into the project, and developed ideas with her.

These brief outlines of several of the individual projects illustrate four key features found in each of them:

1 a coherent sense of purpose;
2 a strong sense of the possible;
3 an openness to new possibilities;
4 an openness to new relationships.

We would suggest that these features are essential in pre-school settings in order for them to deal with the rapidly changing contexts in which they are operating.

Writing about subject departments in secondary schools, Andy Hargreaves (1994) identified two models of departmental structure which seemed best able to deal with the shifting demands facing education professionals: collaborative cultures and moving mosaics. Our own evaluation work in primary schools suggests that collaborative cultures seem to work well in small schools where sharing values and strategies is relatively easy and practitioners can deal collaboratively with changing demands, confident of the support of their colleagues. Larger primary schools, however, need to work at being moving mosaics by encouraging a flexible approach to roles, allowing new roles to develop and be accommodated into existing structures and allowing flexibility of roles at the boundaries of the school and its communities. The moving mosaic of developing roles and sometimes fuzzy boundaries between roles is held together by a strong sense of common purpose. In moving mosaic primary schools, colleagues are able to work responsively when the situation demands it, confident of a strong sense of shared purpose and responsibility. We have argued throughout this text that knowledgeable and responsive action has to lie at the core of being an educare professional and that practitioners need to work in contexts where this kind of action can occur.

The project as a learning network

We designed the project with relationships very firmly in mind. A new knowledge community could not be developed unless relationships across boundaries were possible and new forms of practical knowledge could be generated in joint action. We were influenced in our thinking by the idea of learning networks. We thought that networks would allow participants to bring together the best of current practice, refreshed by external insights, and develop understandings that would allow them to make informed decisions about future practice. In Chapter 3 we discussed cross-settings action research as a powerful vehicle for the generation of the practical knowledge of educare. In this section we look how we operated as a network for learning.

We were aware that our roles as higher education-based researchers in the action research of settings-based practitioners, and in the project as a network, needed exploring. Elliott's (1994) work on teachers' knowledge and action research reminds us of the place of theory and the role of higher education in action research networks. He argues that the ideas of theorists don't threaten practitioners if these ideas can be translated into concrete curriculum proposals that can be scrutinized in action by practitioners who then decide what should be ultimately absorbed into practice. Action research, he suggests, gives the university-based 'theorist' a role as supplier of theoretical resources for practitioners to draw on when analysing and developing practice. However, he emphasizes that the practitioner is the ultimate judge of what is useful knowledge. Elliott's ideas resonate with those of Paul Hirst, who argues that practical reasoning is developed when practice is illuminated by reference to theoretical reasoning (Hirst 1996), and this illumination occurs in conversations about practice.

Elliott's summary of the role of university-based staff in teachers' action research projects is a useful starting point. However, our project as a network did more than simply focus on how individual practitioners developed practical reasoning. Our role involved us in working at three organizational levels: the local authority, the pre-school setting and groups of practitioners. Key stakeholders in each of these levels were crucial to the success of the project and we could not have found ourselves with better collaborators. Each level in turn enabled the next. The senior local authority officers with whom we planned the project shared our vision and identified experienced and responsible stakeholders at the level of the settings and then did all they could to support the activities at settings level. The experienced settings-based staff became our research partners and, in turn, enabled the responsive activities of their colleagues as they worked with new strategies with children and with other agencies or parents.

This strong, multi-level commitment to the project then served as a sound basis for the learning network we established. Learning a new form of professional practice in the acts of practice can be highly challenging. Work on teacher training, for example, suggests that student teachers are strongly resistant to developing new ways of interpreting classroom events and responding to them (Desforges 1995; Edwards 1998). Part of the difficulty lies in the need for them to experience a destabilization of current understandings before new ones are recognized as necessary. The destabilizing can be professionally threatening when working publicly with children.

Going slowly was therefore essential. At Step 1 we gained agreement on (i) the purposes of the project and (ii) that we would work slowly from evidence gathered in the settings. During Step 1 we spent time at workshops, building relationships through sharing current understandings and concerns, and everyone visited each others' settings. We cannot overestimate the importance of the time taken to establish sound relationships across the network. At two residential meetings and workshops at Steps 2 and 3, participants provided each other with both enthusiastic interest in progress and informed support at times of glitch. Mutual support was an extremely important feature and gives us some confidence in the sustainability of the network we helped to establish.

As we mentioned in Chapter 3, our roles changed over the duration of the project as the practitioners gained control of the presentation of knowledge in discussions and written texts. We were working with our own version of what Huberman (1995) describes as an *open collective cycle* for the generation of changes in the practices of teaching. Huberman's notion of a networked learning cycle is based on the idea of collaboration between several schools which share a common pedagogic focus for their activities. Huberman's cycle is managed by the group of schools which calls in external specialists when required. These external specialists may be from higher education or they may be other specialists. Their roles include what he terms 'conceptual inputs', 'experience sharing', 'help with observations of practice' and the 'analysis of observations'.

Our conceptual inputs were most overt in Step 1 when we ran the topic-based workshops and produced the research summaries we outlined in Chapter 3, and they continued in discussions about practice in Steps 2 and 3. However, conceptual framings were increasingly represented in the contexts of practice by our research partners who appropriated the frameworks we shared and used them in discussions of practice. Experience sharing occurred regularly in workshops and, as we visited each setting, we carried information about developments from one setting to another and shared experiences and practical ideas we had gained elsewhere in similar projects. Help with observations came through advice on observational methods for both exploring practice (see Chapter 3) and formatively assessing children (see Chapter 8). Analysis of observations also occurred during our visits and in workshops. By Step 3, most settings were managing their own evaluations of their work in their own settings.

We saw the network as a set of overlapping communities of practice, all with the interests of children as learners as a central concern. As researchers we belonged primarily to the research community. Our research partners were primarily practitioners, who themselves belonged to the communities of, for example, either care or education. The senior managers were led by the concerns of that role. We all brought a range of strengths and experiences to the project. We learnt from each other as we moved in and out of the overlapping communities, gathering information and sharing insights drawn from our particular expertise.

What did we two researchers learn? We started the project with a strong belief in the shared wisdom of the people with whom we were working. We learnt very quickly not to underestimate their thirst for information and the capacity to take that information into practice for professional scrutiny. Most importantly, our view that educare was more about the development of informed and responsive professionals than about the creation of a curriculum, was substantiated every time we spoke to any of our research partners.

But was educare as a community of practice established through the project? Responses to the questionnaire we discussed in Chapter 3 suggest that only one of the key practitioners thought so. However, the rest were unanimous in thinking that we had, between us, established a community of understanding which would serve to underpin future developments in educare. Given our emphasis on professional practice as informed responsive decision making we were considerably heartened by these responses.

 Contexts for the development of educare

An informed professional can only work responsively in a context that allows this to happen. This does not mean that professionals are victims of the systems in which they find themselves operating. Neither does it mean that an individual in isolation can change a system and what is allowed to occur within it. Educare professionals, working together, need to see the possibilities for informed responsive action that are available to them in their settings, and use those possibilities. They need to talk about what they are doing and why they are doing it and so take responsibility for the generation of their own knowledge base.

The development of educare will depend upon the continuous development, in action, of a common store of practical knowledge which is itself constantly open to scrutiny. Such scrutiny can only occur in a professional climate that encourages the confidence to value openness and collaboration across boundaries of profession and location so that the best interests of children are served.

 ## Suggested reading

See Dahlberg, G. and Åsén, G. (1994) 'Evaluation and regulation: a question of empowerment', in P. Moss and A. Pence (eds) *Valuing Quality in Early Childhood Services* (London: Paul Chapman) for a discussion of the cultural conditions for the renewal of early childhood education, which argues that policies for children and youth need to be serious areas of discussion for a wide range of stakeholders.

Hawkins, P. and Shohet, R. (1989) *Supervision in the Helping Professions* (Buckingham: Open University Press) is an excellent and accessible distillation of research and advice on supervision and leadership which aims at professional development.

Rodd, J. (1994) *Leadership in Early Childhood* (Buckingham: Open University Press) is a useful compilation of research on leadership and team building geared towards early years practice.

Blenkin, G. and Kelly, A.V. (eds) (1997) *Principles into Practice in Early Childhood Education* (London: Paul Chapman) explores practitioners' ideas about quality in early years practice and begins to discuss the potential of action research for the development of good quality practice. At the time of going to press their follow-up text in which they discuss the action research is not available. However, discussion of their action research projects is available in Blenkin, G. and Hutchin, V. (1998) 'Action Research, child observation and professional development: some evidence from a research project' (*Early Years*, 19 (1) (Autumn): 62–75).

Edwards, A. and Brunton, D. (1993) 'Supporting reflection in teachers' learning', in J. Calderhead and P. Gates (eds) *Conceptualising Reflection in Teacher Development* (London: Falmer) provides a framework for linking action research processes to professional learning, drawing on aspects of the sociocultural frameworks for learning we have been using in the present text.

Elliott, J. (1998) *The Curriculum Experiment: Meeting the Challenge of Social Change* (Buckingham: Open University Press) concludes with a chapter entitled 'What have we learnt from action research?'. Elliott is one of the leading proponents of teacher-led curricular and pedagogic change in the UK and in this chapter draws on the work of Tony Giddens (1984) to discuss action research and the complex relationship between individual agency and organizational structures.

⑩ Early childhood services in the new millennium

○ Policy changes

In the final year of the project policy changes were still coming thick and fast from central government. The thrust of policy was towards establishing comprehensive and integrated childhood services for the families of the new millennium.

In May 1998 the government published a Green Paper, *Meeting the Childcare Challenge* (DfEE 1998b), outlining a strategy for ensuring good quality, affordable child care for children aged 0 to 14. Early Years Development Partnerships in local authorities were expanded to include this much wider remit and renamed Early Years Development and Childcare Partnerships. Partnerships were required to audit current provision for child care in their authorities and to prepare child care development plans. The New Deal for the Unemployed and New Deal for Lone Parents intiatives were set up to support those wishing to return to work or training. A 'working families' tax credit' was introduced to help parents with child care costs. Policy makers grappled with how best to combine the inspections currently operated separately by Ofsted and by local authorities under the 1989 Children Act regulations into one coherent system. Partnership committees were invited to respond to a consultation paper on rationalizing the distinct operations of care and educational settings. Thus, child care was seen as an aid to address regeneration, social exclusion, crime prevention, and educational and health issues. A tall order indeed, but one that puts early childhood workers at the heart of social policy initiatives as we head for the new millennium.

In 1998 it was announced that the entitlement of 4-year-olds to pre-school places was to be extended to 66 per cent of 3-year-olds (where parents want to take them up). By 2002 the government expects an extra 190,000 3-year-olds to be in nurseries or playgroups. This may mean offering financial support to the Pre-School Learning Alliance to encourage them to reopen some of the playgroups which did not survive loss of income when their 4-year-olds drifted into primary schools under the voucher initiative in 1996.

In 1999 an initiative called Surestart was launched to support parents of children up to the age of 3 where families are struggling with poverty and deprivation. Some 250 centres will be set up over a three-year period. Margaret Hodge, the minister with responsibility for the Surestart initiative said that the centres would be 'within pram-pushing distance and the services provided will be universal in the area covered by the project. All parents of new babies will be visited and made aware of what professional services or other services are available' (*Times Educational Supplement* 1998). Programmes based at the centres will be managed jointly by education and health services. Surestart is one plank of the government strategy to coordinate the work of agencies to tackle family problems which may have multiple causes related to health, employment, housing, education and welfare. The long-term aim is to tackle the underlying causes of underachievement in education and of social exclusion within families and communities. Surestart initiatives will link with 'education action zones' designed to inject positive programmes into areas perceived as being educationally disadvantaged. It is likely that Surestart programmes will also be linked to some of the centres of excellence, funded to demonstrate and promote good practice in the integration and multi-agency support of early education and childcare, family services and training.

In 1999 the Qualifications and Curriculum Authority (QCA) proposed two major initiatives with implications for early childhood services. One was the overhaul of the *Desirable Outcomes for Learning* (DfEE/SCAA 1996a) targets for children aged 5. A new curriculum, for the 'Foundation Stage', was drawn up outlining goals for children as they enter Key Stage One at 5. There was an emphasis on literacy and numeracy, in line with the government drive to raise standards in 'the basics', but the goals also acknowledge the importance of informal, play-based learning in promoting young children's communication and social skills. As the book goes to press arguments are raging about the prescriptive nature of the goals and the links made in the consultation document with the national literacy and numeracy stategies.

A new curriculum framework, *Quality in Diversity*, was created by the Early Childhood Forum (1998), based on work done by a project team at Goldsmiths' College in London. The QCA have referenced the framework as having had considerable influence on their rethinking of the foundation curriculum. Drawing on the New Zealand early childhood curriculum, *Te Whariki* (MoE 1993), *Quality in Diversity* has three main elements: foundations (five ideas which are integral to worthwhile learning in the early years); goals (detailed descriptions of what the foundations mean in terms of children's learning); and children's entitlements (to ensure that the foundations are firmly established in every setting). The titles of the foundations – belonging and connecting, being and becoming, contributing and participating, being active and expressing and thinking, imagining and understanding – are very unlike the headings for the subject-orientated foundation stage goals.

The second major initiative from the QCA was to establish a framework for qualifications and training to meet the staffing needs of the massive expansion in services for children under 14. A consultation paper, *A Draft Framework for Qualifications and Training in the Early Years Education, Childcare and Playwork Sector*, was published by the QCA in November 1998. The aim was to have a framework for qualifications and training for childcare workers in place by 1999 so that much of the training starting in September of that year would conform to national standards. The framework will ensure that educare workers can equip themselves to work cross-sector. Seven broad occupational groups have been identified:

1 early years development and child care;
2 playwork;
3 sports, recreation and activity leadership;
4 youth work;
5 working with families;
6 in-school and out-of-school study and learning support;
7 work in health-related fields.

Section 2.31 of the consultation paper talks of 'a climbing frame' to help people enter, move and progress in the sector, as well as to move to other related occupations. Links will be made with teaching, social work and nursing qualifications.

A Green Paper has been published on qualifications for the teaching profession, *Teachers Meeting the Challenge of Change* (DfEE 1998a), which reviews training arrangements for those planning to work with young children. It is worrying that the only reference to early years teacher training includes statements about upgrading nursery nurse and teaching assistants qualifications such as: 'Nursery nurses play a particularly valuable role in the education of young children, often working in a team with the teacher in a nursery class' and 'For teaching assistants . . . a modular approach with a core set of competences which would be recommended for most assistants and then specialist modules for those working on specific areas such as literacy or numeracy, or supporting pupils with special educational need'. There is also a reference to making it easier for teaching assistants to become qualified teachers (DfEE 1998a: 53, para. 137). The qualifications will also link-in with the growing number of childhood studies degrees and postgraduate diplomas being set up in universities across the country. But if we are to rethink teaching qualifications for early childhood settings we must recognize that the nature of teaching is changing. The current emphasis on subject knowledge in teacher training programmes at the expense of time allocated to understanding how children learn and develop is unhelpful. Yet we should be wary of condoning qualifications to teach young children which do not retain appropriate graduate status, rates of pay and conditions of service for those opting to train to teach young children.

A recent publication by Oberhuemer and Ulich (1997) documents the major kinds of provision for young children in a range of European countries and in Scandanavia, and describes the kinds of training and qualifications required for child care work in each country. The expectation is that European workers may be far more mobile when seeking employment in the future. For the generation of young educare workers entering the new millennium it may be quite normal for them to seek work in other countries for periods of their working lives and there is likely to be some international agreement on what qualifications are transferable for work with young children in different sectors.

Both the foundation curriculum and training initiatives will involve grass-roots practitioners and training agencies having to cope with yet more change. But, as we pointed out at the end of Chapter 1, settings for young children in the UK were always likely to look very different in ten years time. In their book *Transforming Nursery Education*, Moss and Penn (1996) promote an exciting vision of integrated services for young children and their families in the future. At the end of the book they describe three very different examples of how workplaces might be: a community centre nursery, a school campus, and a nursery school and out-of-school club set in a park. These examples are illustrative of Moss and Penn's vision of 'a comprehensive, integrated and coherent early childhood service, flexible and multi-functional . . . a rich and enhancing experience for everyone involved in it – children first and foremost, but also parents, staff, members of the local community' (p. 165).

Policy into practice: working towards a community of practice

Policy changes at the outer, macro-level, of systems can seem oppressive to those struggling to implement them at the micro-level of their workplaces. Yet Bronfenbrenner's (1979) model allocates to both children and the adults working with them an active role in shaping their own practices and behaviours within the various levels so that they in turn can impact from the inside outwards and influence policy makers. Certainly taking a proactive rather than reactive stance in managing change makes workers feel less like the victims of circumstances beyond their control. But, as we have argued, practitioners need support at critical times to enable them to face up to and manage change.

The model we adopted in the project reported in this book was to set up cross-sector and cross-authority learning networks in the exo- and meso-systems surrounding the practitioners' workplaces. We learned how important these networks were in sustaining the momentum for coping with change. It is very hard for practitioners to persevere at analysis of their practice in their own workplaces without the incentive of sympathetic listeners, feedback gained from sharing their ideas with critical but informed others and reassurance that their work is valued. We were working towards establishing a community of practice of informed educarers which would survive the immediate aims of the project. In fact, not only did these networks sustain innovation during the project but they have led to several other sub-groups forming and re-forming for secondary professional purposes within the local authorities. In some cases the support systems have encouraged individuals to change career aspirations or study for degree- or Masters-level qualifications. So the aspiration to influence others out there beyond the micro-system level has been realized by members of the project networking beyond their workplaces.

A second crucial principle was that dialogue between members of the community of practice was based on documentary evidence of the realities of their everyday working lives. The action research model provided a demanding but rewarding structure by which we were all required to centre our dialogues on analysis of obervations, fieldnotes, photographs, video recordings, children's models and drawings and the conversations of parents and staff. Only by focusing on these realities and developing a culture of collaboration rather than confrontation could we move forward and begin to develop a discourse that bridged the gaps we encountered between the working realities and priorities of the university, day care, playgroup, school and childminding worlds.

It became increasingly obvious that we needed to bridge another set of gaps – those between practitioners and parents. We learnt that it was often through discussing cultural tools (children's drawings, scrapbooks, profile notes) when engaging parents in dialogue about their children that we began to recognize the significance of these objects as the stimuli for meaningful exchanges across the gaps. In contrast, formal meetings set up to transmit 'professional knowledge' to parents often foundered.

We learnt that communication across all manner of gaps was only likely to be at a deep rather than superficial level if it recognized rather than repressed differences in people's views of children and their needs and used the differences as the creative starting point for meaningful exchanges of ideas. We were all catapulted outside our own safe worlds of work both literally and metaphorically. For some practitioners, coming into a university workplace setting for meetings was intimidating, and for the researchers complex journeys across three large local authority areas in search of day care or nursery workplace settings forced them to confront anxieties of their own about how they would cope with unfamiliar people and places. Many of us were juggling domestic with professional responsiblities. We all stepped out of domestic realities into living together in the unfamiliar surroundings of a hotel and a hall of residence for two residentials. None of this was easy. It required taking risks and risking loss of face for every one of the project team at some point as we worked together to co-construct our community of practice.

 ## A knowledge base for educarers

Project members came from a range of different types of settings. The foci for sharing our knowledge as practitioners in this project were literacy and mathematical thinking, but the skills we acquired in researching and making explicit what knowledge we carried within our practice were transferable to other areas of learning. We could have gained as much from focusing on knowledge and understanding of the world or on creative activities, for example. An important principle was that it was the starting point of analysing episodes of children and adults learning together in real settings that gave our dialogues authenticity and depth. When we tracked episodes of literacy and mathematical learning in settings, there was evidence that much valuable learning was happening within the everyday activities of the daily play and domestic routines. It came as a surprise to many of the group that there was so much wisdom in their current practice. Careful analysis of those episodes prompted us to want to make much more of what we were already doing. So, for example, practitioners did not want to buy expensive new equipment or resources but they wanted to make much better informed use of what they already had. Over and over again we came back to the conviction that though we were quite good at planning activities and matching resources to intended learning outcomes, we were less certain about the quality of adult and children's learning behaviours when the paper plans were translated into action.

Sometimes the hardest task was to put implicit knowledge into words. Project members groaned at our requests that they write down what they had learned from their action research in order to make that knowledge explicit for a wider audience. Having once grasped the nettle, at our last residential together, the team were adamant when they reviewed the accumulated papers outlining the individual projects, that they wanted to publish accounts of the research and analysis they had done. As they rightly argued, others reading their guidelines for literacy and mathematical thinking for young children would need to understand the processes by which they had come to their models. They did not want to publish a set of 'tips' for practitioners.

To their great credit, though they expressed clearly at the start of the project that they were less confident in their grasp of mathematical learning, many of the team took the risk of focusing on mathematics for their action research cycle. By the end of the project the repertory grid exercise indicated that though they still felt less confident in their grasp of mathematics than literacy learning, nevertheless they had developed a greater 'at homeness' with number. Their confidence in managing children's learning in literacy had developed considerably. Though putting what they knew in writing had been demanding, they acknowledged that it had helped them to clarify their own understanding. When we shared all the project materials at the final residential they gained confidence from the realization that their professional knowledge both as individuals and as a community was impressive. Thus in articulating their understanding of how children learnt, they had themselves taken great strides as learners.

Again and again we returned to the notion of the significance of the quality of interactions between adults and children and adults and adults in the workplace as at the heart and soul of good professional practice. A phrase that had initially seemed abstract and intimidating to the group, 'joint involvement episodes', became a kind of mantra for the team when we focused on the 'pedagogy' of working with young children. We also recognized the importance of the degree of intimacy and emotional engagement between adults and children if they were to be meaningful to both parties. We recognized the importance of structuring high quality learning opportunities – sharing books, setting up lively construction play areas, making music, making meaning through art work, models or role play. But we became more and more convinced of the importance of adults following children's learning by careful observation as the precursor to leading children, through guided participation, towards new learning. Early years practitioners and researchers need to substantiate this approach with robust research evidence to counter the 'colonization' of home and pre-school settings by the educational dogma of direct instruction.

Our hope is that the kind of collaboration between higher education-based researchers, local authority officers and early years practitioners exemplified in the project on which this book was based will fire others with enthusiasm and intellectual curiosity to explore the complexity within the daily lives of young children and the adults who love, work and play with them. Only by those who care explaining to others how it is will the world of early childhood come to be valued as it should be.

Bibliography

Anning, A. (1994) Play and the legislated curriculum: back to basics, an alternative view, in J. Moyles (ed.) (1994) *The Excellence of Play*. Buckingham: Open University Press.

Anning, A. (1997) *First Years at School*, 2nd edn. Buckingham: Open University Press.

Anning, A. (1999) Learning to draw and drawing to learn, *Journal of Art and Design Education*, 18(2): 163–72.

Athey, C. (1990) *Extending Thought in Young Children: A Parent-Teacher Partnership*. London: Paul Chapman.

Aubrey, C. (1997a) *Mathematics Teaching in the Early Years*. London: Falmer.

Aubrey, C. (1997b) Children's early learning of number in school and out, in I. Thompson (ed.) *Teaching and Learning Early Number*. Buckingham: Open University Press.

Audit Commission (1997) *Counting to Five*. Abingdon: Audit Commission Publications.

Baghban, M. (1984) *Our Daughter Learns to Read and Write*. Newark, DE: International Reading Association.

Ball, C. (1994) *Start Right: The Importance of Early Learning*. London: Royal Society of Arts.

Baroody, A.J. (1987) *Children's Mathematical Thinking*. New York: Teachers College Press.

Baroody, A.J. (1993) Fostering the mathematical learning of young children, in B. Spodeck (ed.) *Handbook of Research on the Education of Young Children*. New York: Macmillan.

Bartholemew, L. and Bruce, T. (1993) *Getting to Know You: A Guide to Record-Keeping in Early Childhood Education and Care*. London: Hodder & Stoughton.

BEAM (1997) *Learning Mathematics in the Early Years: Desirable Approaches*. London: BEAM/Early Childhood Mathematics Group.

Bennett, N. and Kell, J. (1989) *A Good Start: Four Year Olds in Infant Schools*. Oxford: Basil Blackwell.

Berliner, D. and Calfee, R. (1996) (eds) *Handbook of Educational Psychology*. New York: Macmillan.

Bissex, G.L. (1980) *GNYS AT WRK: A Child Learns to Read and Write*. London: Harvard University Press.

Blenkin, G. and Hutchin, V. (1998) Action research, child observations and professional development: some evidence from a research project, *Early Years*, 19(1) (Autumn): 62–75.

Blenkin, G.M. and Kelly, A.V. (eds) (1996) *Early Childhood Education: A Developmental Curriculum*, 2nd edn. London: Paul Chapman.

Blenkin, G. and Kelly, A.V. (eds) (1997) *Principles into Practice in Early Childhood Education*. London: Paul Chapman.

Book Trust (1998) *A Gift For Life: Bookstart, Fifth Year*. London: Book Trust.

Bowlby, J. (1953) *Child Care and the Growth of Love*. Harmondsworth: Penguin.

Bradley, M. (1982) *The Coordination of Services for Children Under Five*. Windsor: NFER/Nelson.

Brannan, J. and Moss, P. (1990) *Managing Mothers: Dual Earner Households After Maternity Leave*. London: Unwin Hyman.

Bremner, G. (1994) *Infancy*. Oxford: Blackwell.

Bronfenbrenner, U. (1979) *The Ecology of Human Development: Experiments by Nature and Design*. Cambridge, MA: Harvard University Press.

Brooks, G., Gorman, T., Harman, J., Hutchison, D. and Wilkin, A. (1996) *Family Literacy Works: The NFER Evaluation of the Basic Skills Agency's Demonstration Programmes*. London: Basic Skills Agency.

Bruner, J.S. (1963) *The Process of Education*. New York: Vintage.

Bruner, J.S. (1983) *Child's Talk: Learning to Use Language*. Oxford: Oxford University Press.

Bruner, J.S. (1996) *The Culture of Education*. Cambridge, MA: Harvard University Press.

Bryant, P.E. and Bradley, L. (1985) *Children's Reading Difficulties*. Oxford: Blackwell.

Campbell, R. and Olson, D. (1990) Children's thinking, in R. Grieve and M. Hughes (eds) *Understanding Children*. Oxford: Blackwell.

Chaiklin, S. and Lave, J. (eds) (1993) *Understanding Practice: Perspectives on Activity and Context*. Cambridge: Cambridge University Press.

Chomsky, N. (1976) *Reflections on Language*. London: Fontana.

Clay, M. (1975) *What Did I Write?* London: Heinemann Educational Books.

Cleave, S. and Brown, S. (1989) *Meeting their Needs*. Windsor: NFER/Nelson.

Cleave, S. and Brown, S. (1991a) *Four Year Olds in Infant Classes*. Windsor: NFER/Nelson.

Cleave, S. and Brown, S. (1991b) *Quality Matters*. Windsor: NFER/Nelson.

Cobb, P. and Yackel, E. (1998) A constructivist perspective on the culture of the mathematics classroom, in F. Seeger, J. Voigt and U. Waschescio (eds) *The Culture of the Mathematics Classroom*. Cambridge: Cambridge University Press.

Cockcroft, W.H. (1982) *Mathematics Counts: Report of the Committee of Enquiry into the Teaching of Mathematics in Schools*. London: HMSO.

Cohen, B. and Hagen, U. (1997) *Children's Services: Shaping Up for the Millennium, Supporting Children and Families in the UK and Scandinavia*. Edinburgh: The Stationery Office Limited.

Cole, M., Engestrom, Y. and Vasquez, O. (eds) (1997) *Mind, Culture and Activity.* Cambridge: Cambridge University Press.

Cooter, R. (ed.) (1992) *In the Name of the Child.* London: Routledge.

Dahlberg, G. and Åsén, G. (1994) Evaluation and regulation: a question of empowerment, in P. Moss and A. Pence (eds) *Valuing Quality in Early Childhood Services.* London: Paul Chapman.

Dahlberg, G., Moss, P. and Pearce, A. (1999) *Beyond Quality in Early Childhood Education and Care: Postmodern Perspectives.* London: Falmer Press.

David, T. (ed.) (1993) *Educational Provision for our Youngest Children.* London: Paul Chapman.

David, T. (ed.) (1998) *Researching Early Childhood Education: European Perspectives.* London: Paul Chapman.

David, T., Curtis, A. and Siraj-Blatchford, I. (1993) *Effective Teaching in the Early Years: Fostering Children's Learning in Nurseries and in Infant Classes,* an OMEP (UK) report. Warwick: University of Warwick for Organisation Mondiale pour l'Education Prescolaire.

De Corte, E., Greer, B. and Verschaffel, L. (1996) Mathematics teaching and learning, in D. Berliner and R. Calfee (eds) *Handbook of Educational Psychology.* New York: Macmillan.

DES (Department of Education and Science) (1972) *Education: A Framework for Expansion* (White Paper), Cmnd 5174. London: HMSO.

DES (Department of Education) (1988) *National Curriculum Task Group on Assessment and Testing: A Report.* London: HMSO.

DES (Department of Education and Science) (1990) *Starting with Quality. Report of the Committee of Enquiry into the Quality of the Educational Experience Offered to 3 and 4 Year Olds.* London: HMSO.

DES (Department of Education and Science) (1993) *Pupils Under Five Years in Each Local Authority in England – January 1990, Statistical Bulletin 7/93.* London: HMSO.

Desforges, C. (1995) How does experience affect theoretical knowledge for teaching? *Learning and Instruction,* 5(4): 385–400.

DfEE (Department for Education and Employment) (1997) *Excellence in Schools.* London: DfEE.

DfEE (Department for Education and Employment) (1998a) *Teachers Meeting the Challenge of Change* (Green Paper), Cm 4164. London: HMSO.

DfEE (Department for Education and Employment (1998b) *Meeting the Childcare Challenge* (Green Paper). London: HMSO.

DfEE/SCAA (Department for Education and Employment/School Curriculum and Assessment Authority) (1996a) *Desirable Outcomes for Children's Learning on Entering Compulsory Education.* London: DfEE/SCAA.

DfEE/SCAA (Department for Education and Employment/School Curriculum and Assessment Authority) (1996b) *Nursery Education Scheme: The Next Steps.* London: DfEE.

DoH (Department of Health) (1991) *The Children Act 1989: Guidance and Regulations, Volume 2, Day Care and Educational Provision for Young Children.* London: HMSO.

Donaldson, M. (1978) *Children's Minds.* London: Croom Helm.

Dunn, J. (1988) *The Beginnings of Social Understanding.* Oxford: Blackwell.

Early Childhood Forum (1998) *Quality in Diversity in Early Learning: A Framework for Early Childhood Practitioners.* London: National Children's Bureau.

Edwards, A. (1998) Mentoring student teachers in primary schools, *European Journal of Teacher Education*, 21(1): 47–62.

Edwards, A. (1999) Research and practice: is there a dialogue? in H. Penn (ed.) *Theory, Policy and Practice in Early Childhood Services.* Buckingham: Open University Press.

Edwards, A. and Brunton, D. (1993) Supporting reflection in teachers' learning, in J. Calderhead and P. Gates (eds) *Conceptualising Reflection in Teacher Development.* London: Falmer.

Edwards, A. and Knight, P. (1994) *Effective Early Years Education.* Buckingham: Open University Press.

Edwards, A. and Talbot, R. (1999) *The Hardpressed Researcher: A Research Handbook for Education, Health and Social Care*, 2nd edn. London: Longman.

Edwards, C., Gandini, L. and Forman, G. (eds) (1993) *The Hundred Languages of Children: The Reggio Emilia Approach to Early Childhood Education.* Norwood: NJ: Ablex Publishing Company.

Egan, K. (1988) *Primary Understanding: Education in Early Childhood.* London: Routledge.

Elfer, P. and McQuail, S. (1995) *Local Wishes and Expectations.* London: National Children's Bureau.

Elfer, P. and Selleck, D. (1999) *The Best of Both Worlds: Enhancing the Experience of Young Children in the Nursery.* London: National Children's Bureau.

Elfer, P., Goldschmied, E. and Selleck, D. (1999) *Working with Children Under Three: The Keyperson Relationship.* London: National Children's Bureau.

Elliott, J. (1994) Research on teachers' knowledge in action research, *Educational Action Research*, 2(1): 133–7.

Elliott, J. (1998) *The Curriculum Experiment: Meeting the Challenge of Social Change.* Buckingham: Open University Press.

Engeström, Y. (1993) Developmental studies of work as a testbench of activity theory: the case of primary care medical practice, in S. Chaiklin and J. Lave (eds) *Understanding Practice: Perspectives on Activity and Context.* Cambridge: Cambridge University Press.

Ferreiro, E. and Teberovsky, A. (1982) *Literacy Before Schooling.* London: Heinemann Educational Books.

Ferri, E., Birchall, D., Gingell, V. and Gipps, C. (1981) *Combined Nursery Centres: A New Approach to Education and Day Care.* London: Macmillan.

Fransella, F. and Bannister, D. (1977) *A Manual for Repertory Grid Technique.* New York: Academic Press.

Fransella, F. and Thomas, L. (eds) (1988) *Experimenting with Personal Construct Psychology.* London: Routledge.

Frith, U. (1989) *Autism: Explaining the Enigma.* Oxford: Blackwell.

Fromberg, D.P. (1990) An agenda for research on play in early childhood education, in E. Klugman and S. Smilansky (eds) *Children's Play and Learning: Policy Implications.* New York: Columbia University Teachers' College Press.

Fullan, M. (1991) *The New Meaning of Educational Change.* London: Cassell.

Fullan, M. (1993) *Change Forces.* London: Falmer.

Fuson, K. and Hall, J. (1983) The acquisition of early number word meanings: a conceptual analysis and review, in H. Ginsburg (ed.) *The Development of Mathematical Thinking*. New York: Academic Press.

Gelman, R. and Gallistel, C.R. (1986) *The Child's Understanding of Number*. Cambridge, MA: Harvard University Press.

Giddens, A. (1984) *The Constitution of Society*. Cambridge: Polity Press.

Giddens, A. (1994) *The Constitution of Society*. Cambridge: Polity Press.

Giddens, A. (1998) *The Third Way*. Cambridge: Polity Press.

Ginsburg, H. (ed.) (1983) *The Development of Mathematical Thinking*. New York: Academic Press.

Gipps, C. (1994) *Beyond Testing: Towards a Theory of Educational Assessment*. London: Falmer.

Goldschmied, E. and Jackson, S. (1994) *People Under Three*. London: Routledge.

Goswami, U. and Bryant, P.E. (1990) *Phonological Skills and Learning to Read*. London: Lawrence Erlbaum Associates.

Gregory, E. (1996) *Making Sense of a New World: Learning to Read in a Second Language*. London: Paul Chapman.

Gregory, E. (ed.) (1998) *One Child, Many Worlds*: *Early Learning in Multicultural Communities*. London: David Fulton Publishers.

Hall, N. (1987) *The Emergence of Literacy*. Sevenoaks: Hodder & Stoughton.

Hargreaves, A. (1994) *Changing Teachers, Changing Times*. London: Cassell.

Harré, R. (1983) *Personal Being*. Oxford: Blackwell.

Hawkins, P. and Shohet, R. (1989) *Supervision in the Helping Professions*. Milton Keynes: Open University Press.

Heath, S.B. (1982) What no bedtime story means: narrative skills at home and at school, *Language in Society*, 11: 49–75.

Heath, S.B. (1983) *Ways with Words: Language, Life and Work in Communities and Classrooms*. Cambridge: Cambridge University Press.

Hillgate Group (1986) *Whose Schools? A Radical Manifesto*. London: Claridge Press.

Hirst, P. (1996) The demands of professional practice and preparation for teaching, in J. Furlong and R. Smith (eds) *The Role of Higher Education in Initial Teacher Training*. London: Kogan Page.

HMSO (1998) *Meeting the Childcare Challenge*. London: HMSO.

HMSO Education, Arts and Science Committee (1989) *Achievement in Primary Schools*, vol. 1. London: HMSO.

Holtermann, S. (1992) *Investing in Young Children: Costing an Education and Day Care Service*. London: National Children's Bureau.

Holtermann, S. (1995) *Investing in Young Children: A Reassessment of the Cost of an Education and Day Care Service*. London: National Children's Bureau.

Hopkins, D. (1993) *A Teachers' Guide to Classroom Research*, 2nd edn. Buckingham: Open University Press.

Howes, C. (1988) Relations between early child care and schooling, *Developmental Psychology*, 24: 53–7.

Huberman, M. (1995) Networks that alter teaching: conceptualisations, exchanges and experiments, *Teachers and Teaching: Theory and Practice*, 1(2): 193–211.

Hughes, M. and Westgate, D. (1998) Teachers and other adults as talk partners for pupils in nursery and reception classes, in M. Woodhead, D. Faulkner and K. Littleton (eds) *Cultural Worlds of Early Childhood*. London: Routledge.

Hutt, S.J., Tyler, S., Hutt, C. and Christopherson, H. (1989) *Play Exploration and Learning: A Natural History of the Pre-school*. London: Routledge.

Kleinburg, S. and Menmuir, J. (1995) Perceptions of mathematics in prefives settings, *Education*, 3–13 (October): 29–35.

Kress, G. (1997) *Before Writing: Rethinking the Paths to Literacy*. London: Routledge.

Laminack, L. (1991) *Learning with Zachary*. Richmond Hill, Ontario: Scholastic Canada.

Lave, J. and Wenger, E. (1991) *Situated Learning: Legitimate Peripheral Participation*. Cambridge: Cambridge University Press.

Louis, K.S., Marks, H. and Kruse, S. (1996) Teachers' professional communities in restructuring schools, *American Educational Research Journal*, 33(4): 757–98.

Lowndes, V. and Riley, K. (1994) *Coordinating Services for Young Children: The Implication for Management*. London: Local Government Management Board.

McGuire, J., and Richman, N. (1986) The prevalence of behaviour problems in three types of pre-school group, *Journal of Child Psychology and Psychiatry*, 27: 455–72.

Makins, V. (1997) *Not Just a Nursery: Multi-agency Early Years Centres in Action*. London: National Children's Bureau.

Malaguzzi, L. (ed.) (1987) *I Cento Linguaggi dei Bambini [The Hundred Languages of Children] Assessorato all 'istuzione*, Reggio Emilia.

Matthews, J. (1994) *Helping Children to Draw and Paint in Early Childhood: Young Children and Visual Representation*. London: Hodder & Stoughton.

Meadows, S. (1993) *The Child as Thinker*. London: Routledge.

Melhuish, E.C. (1991) Research on day care for young children in the United Kingdom, in E.C. Melhuish and P. Moss (eds) *Day Care for Young Children: International Perspectives*. London: Routledge.

Mercer, N. (1995) *The Guided Construction of Knowledge: Talk Amongst Teachers and Learners*. Clevedon: Multilingual Matters.

Mercer, N. (1996) The quality of children's collaborative talk in the classroom, *Learning and Instruction*, 6(4): 359–77.

Merttens, R. and Vass, J. (1990) *Bringing School Home: Children and Parents Learning Together*. London: Hodder & Stoughton.

Merttens, R. and Vass, J. (eds) (1993) *Partnerships in Maths: Parents and School*. London: Falmer.

Miller, L. (1996) *Towards Reading*. Buckingham: Open University Press.

Mills, C. and Mills, D. (1998) *Britain's Early Years Disaster* (survey of research evidence for Channel 4 television documentary *Too Much, Too Soon*). London: Channel 4 Television.

MoE (Ministry of Education, New Zealand) (1993) *Te Whariki*. Wellington: New Zealand Learning Media.

Montague-Smith, A. (1997) *Mathematics in Nursery Education*. London: David Fulton.

Morgan, P. (1996) *Who Needs Parents? The Effects of Childcare and Early Education on Children in Britain and the USA* (Choice in Welfare Series no. 31). London: Institute of Economic Affairs.

Moss, P. (1992) Perspectives from Europe, in G. Pugh (ed.) *Contemporary Issues in the Early Years*. London: Paul Chapman.

Moss, P. and Pence, A. (eds) (1994) *Valuing Quality in Early Childhood Services*. London: Paul Chapman.

Moss, P. and Penn, H. (1996) *Transforming Nursery Education*. London: Paul Chapman.

Munn, P. (1994a) Perceptions of teaching and learning in pre-school centres, in M. Hughes (ed.) *Perceptions of Teaching and Learning*. Clevedon: MultiLingual Matters.

Munn, P. (1994b) The early development of literacy and numeracy skills, *European Early Childhood Research Journal*, 2(1): 5–18.

Munn, P. (1997a) Children's beliefs about counting, in I. Thompson (ed.) *Teaching and Learning Early Number*. Buckingham: Open University Press.

Munn, P. (1997b) Writing and number, in I. Thompson (ed.) *Teaching and Learning Early Number*. Buckingham: Open University Press.

Munn, P. and Schaffer, H.R. (1993) Literacy and numeracy events in social interactive contexts, *International Journal of Early Years Education*, 1(3): 61–80.

NATE (National Association of Teachers of English) (1998) *NATE Position Paper No. 3: Literacy*. Sheffield: National Association of Teachers of English.

National Commission on Education (1993) *Learning to Succeed: A Radical Look at Education Today and a Strategy for the Future*. London: Heinemann.

Newson, J. and Newson, E. (1975) Intersubjectivity and the transmission of culture, *The Bulletin of the British Psychological Society*, 28: 437–46.

Nunes, T. and Bryant, P. (1996) *Children Doing Mathematics*. Oxford: Blackwell.

Oberhuemer, P. and Ulich, M. (1997) *Working with Young Children in Europe: Provision and Staff Training*. London: Paul Chapman.

Ogden, L. (1997) *Processes of collaboration in the infant school classroom: their nature and the effects of task structure*. Unpublished PhD thesis, University of Leeds.

Oppenheim, A.N. (1992) *Questionnaire Design, Interviewing and Attitude Measurement*. London: Pinter.

Osborn, A.F. and Milbank, J.E. (1987) *The Effects of Early Education: A Report from the Child Health and Education Study*. Oxford: Oxford University Press.

Paley, V.S. (1986) On listening to what the children say, *Harvard Educational Review*, 56: 122–30.

Pascal, C. (1990) *Under-Fives in Infant Classrooms*. Stoke-on-Trent: Trentham Books.

Pascal, C., Bertram, T. and Ramsden, F. (1997) The effective early learning research project: reflections upon the action during phase 1, *Early Years*, 17(2): 40–7.

Penn, H. (1999) (ed.) *Theory, Policy and Practice in Early Childhood Services*. Buckingham: Open University Press.

Phillips, T. (1985) Beyond lipservice: discourse development after the age of nine, in G. Wells and J. Nicholls (eds) *Language and Learning: An Instructional Perspective*. Lewes: Falmer.

Pugh, G. (1988) *Services for Under Fives: Developing a Co-ordinated Approach*. London: National Children's Bureau.

Pugh, G. (1996a) A policy for early childhood services, in G. Pugh (ed.) *Contemporary Issues in the Early Years*, 2nd edn. London: Paul Chapman for the National Children's Bureau.

Pugh, G. (1996b) A vision for early childhood services: challenges and opportunities. Paper delivered at the National Children's Bureau conference 'The Future Shape of Early Years Services', London, February.

Pugh, G. and McQuail, S. (1995) *Effective Organisation of Early Childhood Services: Summary and Strategic Framework*. London: Early Childhood Unit/National Children's Bureau Report.

QCA (Qualifications and Curriculum Authority) (1998) *A Draft Framework for Qualifications and Training in the Early Years Education, Childcare and Playwork Sector*. London: Qualifications and Curriculum Authority.

QCA (Qualifications and Curriculum Authority) (1999) *The Review of the Desirable Outcomes*. London: Qualifications and Curriculum Authority.

Rodd, J. (1994) *Leadership in Early Childhood*. Buckingham: Open University Press.

Rogoff, B. (1990) *Apprenticeships in Thinking: Cognitive Development in Social Context*. New York: Oxford University Press.

Rogoff, B. (1991) Social interaction as apprenticeship in thinking: guided participation in spatial planning, in L. Resnick, J. Levine and S. Teasley (eds) *Perspectives on Socially Shared Cognition*. Washington: APA.

Rouse, D. (1990) The first three years of life: children trusting, communicating and learning, in D. Rouse (ed.) *Babies and Toddlers, Carers and Educators: Quality for Under Threes*. London: National Children's Bureau.

Saxe, G., Guberman, S. and Gearhart, M. (1987) *Social Processes in Early Number Development*. Monographs of the Society for Research in Child Development, serial no. 216, vol. 52, no. 2.

Schaffer, H.R. (1992) Joint involvement episodes as contexts for cognitive development, in H. McGurk (ed.) *Childhood and Social Development: Contemporary Perspectives*. Hove: Lawrence Erlbaum.

Schaffer, H.R. (1996) *Social Development*. Oxford: Blackwell.

Schweinhart, L. and Weikart, D. (1993) *A Summary of Significant Benefits: The High Scope Perry Pre-School Study Through Age 27*. Ypsilanti, MI: The High Scope Press.

Scollon, R. and Scollon, B.K. (1981) *Narrative, Literacy and Face in Inter Ethnic Communication*. New York: Ablex.

Seeger, F., Voigt, J. and Waschescio, U. (1998) (eds) *The Culture of the Mathematics Classroom*. Cambridge: Cambridge University Press.

Sharp, C. and Davis, C. (1997a) *Parents' Views of Pre-School: Making Choices*. Slough: NFER.

Sharp, C. and Davis, C. (1997b) *Parents' Views of Pre-School: Quality Matters*. Slough: NFER.

Shorrocks, D., Frobisher, L., Nelson, N., Turner, L. and Waterson, A. (1993) *Implementing National Curriculum Assessment in the Primary School*. London: Hodder & Stoughton.

Stake, R. (1994) Case studies, in N. Denzin and Y. Lincoln (eds) *Handbook of Qualitative Research*. Thousand Oaks, CA: Sage.

Strongin Dodds, L. (1994) Learning together: programmes for parents, *Coordinate*, 39: 12–13.

Sylva, K. (1994) School influences on children's development, *Journal of Child Psychology and Psychiatry*, 35(1): 135–70.

Sylva, K. (1997) The early years curriculum: evidence based proposals. Paper presented at the SCAA conference 'Developing the Primary Curriculum: The Next Steps'. London: SCAA.

Sylva, K. and Moss, P. (1992) *Learning Before School, NCE Briefing No. 8* (November). London: National Commission on Education.

Sylva, K. and Wiltshire, J. (1993) The impact of early learning on children's later development: a review prepared for the RSA inquiry 'Start Right', *European Early Childhood Research Journal*, 1(1): 17–40.

Sylva, K., Roy, C. and Painter, M. (1980) *Childwatching at Playgroup and Nursery School*. London: Grant McIntyre.

Thompson, I. (ed.) (1997) *Teaching and Learning Early Number*. Buckingham: Open University Press.

Times Educational Supplement (1998) Surestart, 20 November: 5.

Trevarthen, C. (1977) Descriptive analyses of infant communicative behaviour, in H.R. Schaffer (ed.) *Studies in Mother Infant Interaction*. London: Academic Press.

Trevarthen, C. (1993) The functions of emotions in early infant communication and development, in J. Nadel and L. Camaiori (eds) *New Perspectives on Early Communicative Development*. London: Routledge.

Tyler, S. (1985) *Keele Pre-School Assessment Guide*. Windsor: National Foundation for Educational Research/Nelson.

Wade, B. (1993) Story at home and school, *Educational Review: Occasional Publications, no. 10*, Birmingham: University of Birmingham.

Weinberger, J., Hannon, P. and Nutbrown, C. (1990) *Ways of Working with Parents to Promote Literacy Development*. Sheffield: University of Sheffield Division of Education.

Wells, G. (1981) *Learning Through Interaction: The Study of Language Development*. Cambridge: Cambridge University Press.

Wells, G. (1985) *Language Development in the Pre-school Years*. Cambridge: Cambridge University Press.

Wells, G. (1987) *The Meaning Makers: Children Learning Language and Using Language to Learn*. London: Heinemann Educational.

Wertsch, J. (1991) A sociocultural approach to socially shared cognition, in L. Resnick, J. Levine and S. Teasley (eds) *Perspectives on Socially Shared Cognition*. Washington: APA.

Wertsch, J. (1997) Collective memory: issues from a sociocultural perspective, in M. Cole, Y. Engestrom and O. Vasquez (eds) *Mind, Culture and Activity*. Cambridge: Cambridge University Press.

Wertsch, J., Del Rio, P. and Alvarez, A. (eds) (1995) *Sociocultural Studies of Mind*. Cambridge: Cambridge University Press.

Whalley, M. (1994) *Learning to be Strong*. London: Hodder & Stoughton.

Whitebrook, M., Howes, C. and Phillips, D. (1989) *Who cares? Child Care Teachers and the Quality of Care in America*. Final Report of the National Child Care Staffing Study, Child Care Employee Project. Oakland, CA.

Whitehead, M.R. (1990) *Language and Literacy in the Early Years: An Approach for Education Students*. London: Paul Chapman.

Wilkinson, J.E. (1994) *Flagships: An Evaluation/Research Study of Community Nurseries in Strathclyde Region 1989–92*. Glasgow: Department of Education, University of Glasgow.

Wolfendale, S. (1989) *All About Me*. London: National Children's Bureau.

Wood, D. (1986) Aspects of teaching and learning, in M. Richards and P. Light (eds) *Children of Social Worlds*. Cambridge: Polity Press.

Wood, D. (1988) *How Children Think and Learn*. Oxford: Blackwell.

Woodhead, M., Faulkner, D. and Littleton, K. (eds) (1998) *Cultural Worlds of Early Childhood*. London: Routledge.

Author index

Subject index